WHY WE LOOK UP

WHY WE LOOK UP

Making Sense of Our Catholic Faith

ROBERT J. CORMIER

A Crossroad Book
The Crossroad Publishing Company
New York

The Crossroad Publishing Company
481 Eighth Avenue, New York, NY 10001

Copyright © 2003 by Robert J. Cormier

All rights reserved. No part of this book may be reproduced, stored in a retrieval system, or transmitted, in any form or by any means, electronic, mechanical, photocopying, recording, or otherwise, without the written permission of The Crossroad Publishing Company.

Printed in the United States of America

Library of Congress Cataloging-in-Publication Data

Cormier, Robert J.
    Why we look up : making sense of our Catholic faith / Robert J. Cormier.
       p. cm.
    ISBN 0-8245-2120-X (alk. paper)
    1. Catholic Church – Doctrines. 2. Theology, Doctrinal – Popular works. I. Title.
BX1754.C579 2003
282–dc21

                              2003012923

1   2   3   4   5   6   7   8   9   10   10   09   07   06   05   04   03

Contents

Introduction — 11

Part One
HAVING FAITH

Creation Was Signed — 15

We Are Made of the Love of God — 16

Stars and Sand — 17

Why We Look Up — 17

What Is Faith? — 18

How to See for Ourselves the Truth of Our Faith — 19

Faith Fulfills Our Human Nature — 21

The Gifts of Faith — 23

Faith Doesn't Change Things, It Changes How We See Things — 26

Thy Kingdom Come — 27

The Joy Is Just Knowing — 27

The Myth "If Only..." — 28

Contents

The Secret of Happiness: Knowing What We Have When We Have It	30
The Secret of Peace	32
What Having Faith Is All About	33
Why Hard Things Happen	34
Why Hard Things Can Happen: Life Was Meant to Be a Struggle	35
Why Suffering?	36
The Greater the Burden, the Greater the Opportunity	37
When Someone We Love Dies...	37
We Are Never Alone	39
God Frees Us from Having to Do Everything So We Can Do Something	40
You Only Need to Do Your Best	42
Give It Back to God	43
But What About "Ask and You Shall Receive"?	44
Don't Forget to Listen	45
The Best Reason to Pray	46
What Is a Personal Relationship with God?	47
We Judge God Backwards	48

Contents

He Couldn't Love You More	50
We Don't Know Why God Loves Us	51
Why Do Some Grow So Much More Than Others?	53
How Love Grows	55

Part Two
LIVING FAITH

The Life of Faith Is Love	59
What Is Love?	59
Sin Is Selfishness	61
The Golden Rule: Why It Works and How to Make It Work for You	63
The Ten Commandments	64
Greed	66
The Corporal Works of Mercy	68
The Spiritual Works of Mercy	69
The Only Sure Sign of Love	70
There Are Many Ways to Give Up Your Life	71
The More You Put Into It, the More You Appreciate It	72
The Exercise of Faith Strengthens It	73

Contents

No Good Work Is Ever Wasted	74
Faith Is Its Own Reward	75
Love Is Its Own Reward	76
Try to See Things from Others' Point of View	78
Apologizing, Who Looks Bad?	78
So What If I'm the Only One?	79
Love Surpasses Justice	80
God Does Not Keep Score	81
How We Will See Our Sins	82
We Are All Far from the Kingdom of God	83
How "Judge Not, or You Will Be Judged" Really Works	84
Forgiveness Is Understanding	86
Forgiveness Is the Decision Not to Hate	87
Forgiveness Is a Vote of Confidence in Self	88
People Have the Power Over You You Give Them	89
The Charity of Friendship and Love of Family	91
How Many People Can Hold Your Hand?	92
The Religion in Romance	93
We Want Our Feelings to Be Returned	94

Contents

The Difference Between Enjoyment and Idolatry	95
The Difference Between Needs and Desires	96
It Is Balance That Gives Joy	97
The Ingredients of a Great Life	98

Part Three
PRACTICING FAITH

We Were Made to Be a Family	103
The Glory Be	105
The Role of Christ in Christian Faith	106
Five Reasons We Believe That Jesus Rose	107
The Six Symbolisms of the Candle	110
The Cross and the Basics	112
The Four Meanings of the Cross	112
The Life of Christ	113
Comments on the Beatitudes	115
The Our Father	116
Why Do We Hail Mary?	118
The Hail Mary	118
The Spirituality of the Sacraments	119
Five Meanings of Mass	121

Contents

How Mass Re-Presents the Cross	122
Three Liturgical Moments	123
Four Reasons to Come to Church	124
Five Values of Confession	125
Comments on the Calendar	127
How to Have a Really Happy Advent	129
How to Make a Really Good Lent	131
Twelve Reasons to Give Things Up	134
Love the Year	137
A Practical Creed	140
A Daily Prayer	141
About the Author	142

Introduction

Certainly we do look *up*.

Our word for where God lives is also our grandest word for sky.

We look to God in order to understand our life.

We live with our heads up because we are a happy people, freed from shame.

But we need to know why. We need to be able to say why. We live in a time of change and a profusion of opinions. And almost everyone who talks to us seems sure. If we are to keep our heads up in this sea of contradictions, we will need an explanation of our faith that makes sense.

Our explanation needs to do justice to our experience of a God who is as great and good as anything we can conceive, and whose greatness and love are contradicted by nothing, not in nor around us.

Therefore, our explanation must let us understand our life and struggles here on earth, and it must provide us with clear guidance and abounding inspiration.

Our faith can be explained to do this. And it can be explained so that we can see for ourselves the truth that was written into all of our hearts. This way we are free to believe with a confidence that nothing can take from us, and free as well from the latest thing or the oldest.

Such a faith can give us peace, purpose, and joy far beyond anything we could ever find anywhere else. And it will give us a program for living and growing, and a spiritual life that we can share.

This is what the reader should expect to find in this little book.

Part One

HAVING FAITH

Having Faith

Creation Was Signed

Tonight, once you go to bed, before you fall asleep, and it is dark and quiet and there are no distractions, think about the simple fact that you are alive. Say to yourself, "I am" — not "I am this or I am that" but simply "I am" — and think about what you mean when you say it.

Immediately you will realize that you are much more than you can possibly put into words. You can say certain things *about* you, but what you *are*, what you are being a person, is much too much to put into words.

In this same moment, you will realize that you are much too much just to be here. You could not have come from nothing, for nothing, and be headed to nothing. You must have come from somewhere.

This is human experience because, for all intents and purposes, creation was signed. Whenever you look closely at anything, you experience that it was made. This is God's signature on creation. Some say they can see it when they look at the majesty of the mountains. Others say they can see it when they look at the power of the sea. But you can even see the hand of God if you look at your own hand, not the fact that it works but the very fact that it is there. You can see the hand of God best when you look at the thing you know best — yourself.

✠

Another way to experience God: Close your eyes and concentrate on the present, the time which is passing *right now*. This is an effective way to put aside distractions and experience the richness of what it is to be alive, what it is to be a person. It is an effective way to experience the fact that there is more to existence than usually meets the eye.

We Are Made of the Love of God

God is the one being who always was, the only one that just is.

This means that everything else had to be made, *and still must be sustained*. After all, something that does not need to be sustained would exist apart from God.

And where God's power is, God is.

And His power is His love.

The world, therefore, and we, are made of the love of God.

Thus, you can see the love of God just looking at your hand. He is that close. You are that valuable. And your life is that secure.

Stars and Sand

There are more stars in the heavens than there are grains of sand on every beach on the face of the earth. Yet in every single grain of sand there are more atoms than there are stars in the heavens.

Not only does God know what each of the atoms in all of these stars is doing, but He has planned what each has done — interacting with every other — for every second of the billions of years that the universe has been in existence.

God is using all these countless interactions to create the family best suited to share His life, giving that family a share in its own creation, giving an essential role to each of its members. Of these, the earth has already seen approximately 75 billion people come and go. Six billion are alive today.

But God knows each of us intimately. He loves each of us with all His heart. Indeed, He is looking at each of us with love at this very moment. And "each of us" means you.

Why We Look Up

We no longer believe that God is in, or beyond, the heavens.

And still we look up.

We still look up because, when we do, we see more. When we look down we see no more than several square feet, whereas when we look up we are looking at as much of creation as we can see. In this sense we are looking at as much of God as we can see. At the very least we get a better sense of His bigness, if not to say His greatness.

Inasmuch as heaven is where God is, to heaven we also look up.

What Is Faith?

What is faith? In its most developed form, faith is a deeply personal relationship with God. In its simplest form, however, faith is the way we explain our life. Guided by what the human spirit has already decided, the simplest form of this explanation consists of the following three basic ideas:

Heaven: We exist because God, who does not need to be explained, decided to share His life.

Love: We are here, in this world, to participate in our own creation. God is giving each of us the opportunity to become our own person. This is the reason that we are born unformed, unknowing, and utterly self-centered, and we are called to grow. We are called to grow in the faith that inspires the love which makes us more like God, and prepares us to share God's life as richly as we might.

God's plan: In the act of creation, God put into action a plan for everything that would ever happen, including all the events of all of our lives. He did this knowing how we would respond to these events. In this way, we become the people God wants us to be, while, in the process, each of us still becomes our own person.

How to See for Ourselves the Truth of Our Faith

To see for ourselves the truth of our faith all we need do to is to ask ourselves the questions that faith answers, and see how we feel about the answers.

We begin with the most basic question of all:

Where do we come from? Is it possible that everything — the universe out there and also the universe within us — is just here, from nothing, for nothing, and is on its way *to* nothing? Or does it make more sense to us that the world and we were made, made by God?

So why did God make us? Is it possible that we were made for death? Is it possible that we who were made to want life so desperately were given life so that life could be taken away? Or is it not evident that we were made for life, life with God who made us?

Why then are we here, in *this* world? Is it possible that we are here merely to kill time before we go to heaven? Or is it not obvious that we are here for something important? And what is more important than love? And by loving don't we grow in love, and in our likeness to God? And by becoming more like God, aren't we growing in our ability to share His life when finally we see Him face to face? And by this process, isn't God giving us some responsibility for who we are, the chance to become our own person?

So if what we do is so important, why do our lives depend on so much we cannot control? After all, we do not choose our parents, or where we are born, or when, or countless other events that form us as the people we are. Is it possible that God just lets these things happen — that He has left us here at the mercy of luck, or other people's badness, or even our own created weakness? Is it possible that God left us here at the mercy of events that even He does not control?

Another way to look at it: When God made the world, did He know what was going to happen? Did He care? Is it possible He had no plan? And if He did plan the events of our lives knowing how we would respond to them, wouldn't this make us the people He wants us to be while at the same time giving us a role in our own creation?

What do you think?

To ask ourselves the questions that faith answers reveals to us the truth because God knew that we would hear about faith from many people, that most would seem sure, and that often they would contradict one another. Therefore, He knew that unless there were some way for us to see the truth for ourselves, faith would not be possible. For this reason, the truth of faith was written into human nature and will be recognized by anyone who looks for it in the right place.

How precisely do we look for the truth of faith? We ask ourselves the questions that faith answers and *consider the alternative.*

Faith Fulfills Our Human Nature

Faith offers hope, and purpose, and peace. Not to believe offers nothing.

Faith gives us the best life that we can possibly have. Not to believe restrains our joy.

Faith brings out the best in people. Not to believe makes no one better.

Faith fulfills our human nature. And this is itself a sign that what faith says is true.

✣

To believe or not to believe is not like the choice between two loves, two jobs, or two places to live, both of which have wonderful qualities though different. This is a choice between two good things. This is a choice where to choose one good thing is to reject another, and to live with the question of whether we made the right decision.

Faith does not present us with such a choice. Faith offers hope, and purpose, and peace. Not to believe leads to hopelessness, meaninglessness, and misery.

Oh, it is true that faith must be lived out. But even here we are not presented with a choice between two good things.

Faith asks us to let go of the idea that there are certain things we have to have. But not to let go does not mean that we get what we thought we had to have.

Faith asks us to love. But not to love does not give us a life that can satisfy.

Faith asks us to accept what God has sent. But not to accept things doesn't change them. Not to accept leaves us only with anger.

Faith is a better choice.

The Gifts of Faith

Faith gives gifts. It is a way of understanding things that changes the lives of those who possess it.

To believe in heaven frees us from the dread of death, or the need to keep ourselves distracted — never really living — because we cannot face the facts of life.

To believe in heaven frees us from anguish at the death of those we love. Though we may miss them, we know that they have gone to God and are more alive than we are. We also know that one day we will be reunited with them. Thus we are not afraid to love them now.

To believe in heaven lets us dream. Though all of us have our dreams, the day comes when most people have to admit, if only to themselves, that their dreams are not going to come true. This never happens to people of faith. We know that our dreams are going to come true, the only place they ever could.

Knowing that we were made for divine life, we understand that we were made to want divine life. Presumably, we also understand that no worldly thing could ever fill us. This is the reason that to get one thing is to want another. Therefore, though we can and we should work to make our lives and our world better, we need not suffer over any one thing we do not yet have. We need not anguish over any one problem we have not yet solved. We need not suffer envy.

Not seeking more from things than they can give, we can enjoy the things we do have. Our house does not have to be a heavenly mansion. Our house is not in heaven. But if we find love there, it can still be a home. The people in our lives do not need to be perfect. No one is perfect. If, nonetheless, they are trying, they can still be our companions.

To believe in heaven gives us joy. At the very least, it gives us hope.

To believe in love gives us purpose. We know why we are here. We know what we should do. We know that what we do will make an eternal difference.

If we believe that we are here to grow in love, we love. We are free — free from the fear that we are giving more than others — to live the only kind of life that could ever satisfy us. God would not have made us so that we could ever be happy doing what is wrong. Rather He made us so that we can be happy only when we are doing what is right. This is the reason that if we live selfishly we are never satisfied, no matter how much we have, whereas if we live a life of love we are always satisfied, no matter how little we have.

If to grow in faith and love is our goal, we gain control over our lives. We are always in a position to do what we want most of all. This is not true if fame or

Having Faith

fortune is our goal. If something worldly is our goal, we have to hope that the world will cooperate. (Probably it will not.) If, instead, to grow in faith and love is our goal, we can always do what we want, no matter what the world may do. If something goes wrong, we can accept it, and thus our faith will grow. If people offend or disappoint us, we can forgive them, and thus our love will grow.

If we believe in God's plan, we have the best possible reason to accept ourselves for who we are. After all, God's plan for everything is also His plan for each of us. Yes, our life is a struggle, but it is a special struggle that God has given us to form each of us into a special person who will have a place in heaven no one else can fill. Understanding this, we can forgive ourselves for what we cannot yet do or have done and cannot change. No longer do we compare ourselves to others. Indeed, once we recognize that God has put all His love into our making, we can love ourselves for who He made us. This makes possible the sincere love of others.

To believe in God's plan allows us to accept whatever has happened and cannot be changed. We may not yet know why something hard has happened, but we can know that it needed to happen, for the best possible reason. Likewise, to believe in God's plan allows us to accept whatever is happening now and cannot yet be changed.

Since we know that everything that is going to happen — once it has happened and cannot be changed — will also follow God's plan, we can live our lives without fear. If we know that a year from now we are going to be where God wants us to be, what's to fear? If we think the same about our family and friends, we can live without the impossible burden of thinking that everything depends on us. Everything does not depend on us. Everything depends on God. Our job is to do our best, the best we can right now. The rest is up to God and His plan.

To believe in God's plan gives us peace.

Faith Doesn't Change Things, It Changes How We See Things

"I'm not losing a daughter; I'm gaining a son." It is often true. And what looked sad now looks good.

This is how faith works. It doesn't change things. It changes how we see things such that what looked bad now looks good, or at least better.

A problem becomes an opportunity for faith.

Another problem becomes an opportunity for love.

Another thing that we don't have, something we just see from a distance, is information that can help us imagine what life with God will be like.

Thy Kingdom Come

"Thy kingdom come." In other words: "Take us to heaven now."

The basis of joy is the knowledge that we are on our way to life with God, to share divine life itself, and to do so forever.

What could possibly be better?

What could better help us to accept whatever we don't have now? After all, compared with what we will have, what we don't have now couldn't appear less important. And compared with eternity, the time we have to wait is all but over.

Thy kingdom come.

The Joy Is Just Knowing

How would you feel if you knew that you were going to get $100 million for next Christmas? You would be happy *now* — before receiving any money. Just knowing it was coming, you would be overjoyed.

And your joy wouldn't last just a day. You would think about it every day; you would dream about how it was going to be; and this would be the greatest joy of all.

What you didn't have right now wouldn't mean a thing. Indeed, what you didn't have right now would only inspire you to dream.

Well, heaven *is* coming. It is better than $100 million. You might have to wait more than a year or two to get there. But when finally your time has come, heaven is forever.

✣

How would you feel if you knew the exact day you were going to die — even if it was a long way off?

For one thing, you would think of it. You would not be able to pretend that you were not going to die.

For another, knowing you had only so many days, you would strive to live each one to the fullest.

Finally, you would get ready. And you would not wait until that last few years. You would want to make use of all the time you had. You would know you would not please God by waiting.

One more question: Why not get going, and do what you would do differently? After all, the exact day *is* coming.

Life is transitory.

The Myth "If Only..."

How often we hear it: "If only this, then I would be happy." If only I had that job, if only I didn't have this problem, then I would want for nothing.

Having Faith

I would want for nothing for about two weeks. To get one thing is to want another. To solve one problem is to get a new one.

We were made for divine life. Therefore, we were made to want it. Therefore, no earthly thing — no house, car, fame, fortune, or human person — could ever fill us. This is the reason that to get one thing is to want another, to solve one problem is to get a new one.

Once we accept that there will always be something, we will no longer say, "If only...." We will no longer suffer over what we do not have. We will not suffer envy. And, not expecting things to do more for us than they can, we can enjoy things for what they *do* offer.

Almost all of us understand the myth "If only...." And almost all of us think that our "If only..." is different.

It is different because, we say, once we get this, we *know* we will want for nothing. We can't imagine what else we might want.

Of course, we should not expect to know what the next thing will be. Like land beyond the horizon, it does not appear until we reach what we were looking at.

The myth "but":

"Yes, I realize that there will always be something, but . . . this is really important . . . this is for the good of other people . . . this is really the only thing I've ever wanted. . . ."

But who doesn't feel that their thing is uniquely important? But isn't this always the way we say, "If only . . ."?

✠

To *enjoy,* we need to be *in joy.* We need to be people of faith.

✠

Happiness comes only from within. It comes when we are happy with ourselves. It is not possible otherwise. And this alone will do it.

✠

A happy life begins with a happy day. It begins when we know how to be happy *now.*

The Secret of Happiness: Knowing What We Have When We Have It

How often do we hear it: "If only I had known how good I had it. If only I had known. . . ." Yet we remain preoccupied with what we don't have — until we have

Having Faith

lost what we once had. Then we too say it: "If only I had known...."

But we forget. We return to a preoccupation with what we don't have. And, of course, there is always something. Therefore, we are never happy.

But happiness, relative earthly happiness, is possible. It comes from turning the tables on the typical attitude. Instead of dwelling on what we *don't* have, we can dwell on what we *do* have.

We can do this best by imagining how we would feel if we lost what today we take for granted. This should not be difficult. Perhaps we have already been without it. Perhaps we know of someone who doesn't have it now.

Let us imagine we didn't have it. And how we would feel. And how we would feel if we got it back.

If we were starving, oh, how we would long for food.

If we were homeless, oh, how we would feel if suddenly we were taken in.

If we were unable to see, or to walk, we would tell ourselves that if only we could see, or walk, we would never complain about anything else again.

The secret of happiness: knowing what we have when we have it.

Gratitude is a choice. Since even the most fortunate are often unsatisfied, it is clear that gratitude does not come from what we have. It comes from how we look at what we have.

The Secret of Peace

The secret of peace is the knowledge that everything that happens follows God's plan for our eternal good. This means *everything* — the wind that blows, the grass that grows — everything.

God does nothing in a general way. Everything He does has precisely the effect that He intends — right down to the last detail. Everything He does that affects people affects each of them in exactly the way He intended to affect them. This applies also to you and me.

What could better help us to accept any misfortune or to live with any mistake that *we* have made?

What could better help us to accept ourselves for who we are?

What could better help us to live our lives without fear?

The secret of peace: Say to God, "Thy will be done" and mean it.

What Having Faith Is All About

Many people think that having faith means that if I *really* believe that God will help me, He will give me what I want. Such people are always shaken when they do not get what they prayed for, especially when what they prayed for was, in their minds, "good."

But having faith does not mean that if we really believe God will do this, He will do it. Having faith means that we really believe in God, that God *is* God, that He knows what He is doing, and that He gives us what we need whether or not we can see it now.

Many of us have an idea of faith that is not faith but belief in some lesser spirit with whom we negotiate for favors by acknowledging his power. In some cases it is belief that the mind has power of its own.

Faith in God is better. After all, God does know what He is doing, and He always sends us what we need. If this is our faith, we are already prepared for anything that may happen. If this is our faith, we already have the best thing that life can give us — peace.

Some people think that if something hard happens and they accept it, the second time around things should go better. If they have accepted hardship twice, the third time things should go better.... But this is not faith in God, that God is God and that He knows what He is doing — even if we do not. Rather, this attitude is belief in some lesser spirit with whom we negotiate for favors by accepting what he has already sent. Faith means that we trust God even if He sends us more than we thought we could bear or more than seems fair.

Why Hard Things Happen

Why do hard things happen? The answer is always: because God is using them to bring about something good, something that could not have happened as well otherwise, something that is going to be well worth whatever people suffered on account of it.

But since there are countless effects from everything that happens, and these extend indefinitely into the future, we cannot know the whole why about something hard that has happened. Not on earth.

Here on earth, however, we can see some of the reasons hard things happen. Sometimes a hard thing gets us a good thing, and sometimes right away. Sometimes hard things teach us a greater appreciation for good things when finally they come.

Of course, God is always using hard things to teach and form us. Perhaps, in order to form us, God needed us to struggle with powerlessness and pain. Perhaps, in order to make us struggle, He needed us to deal with life's seeming randomness or lack of justice.

What is more, in every hard thing that happens, God is giving us an opportunity for faith in Him and His plan for our lives.

If we accept these opportunities, we need no longer to wonder why. We have made our own explanation.

We do not believe in God's plan because we can always see its wisdom. We believe in God's plan because we believe in God.

Why Hard Things Can Happen: Life Was Meant to Be a Struggle

We are here to do the one and only thing that God could not do for us — to gain some responsibility for the person we will be in heaven, to become in some small way our own person.

But for this to happen we — and therefore the world of which we are a part — had to have been made imperfect. If we had been made perfect, we would already be all that we could be. We could not grow. We could not participate in our creation.

This is the reason that we are born unformed, unknowing, and utterly self-centered. This is the reason we can be hurt, and when we *are* hurt we suffer.

All of this makes life a struggle. But struggle makes us give ourselves to the project of our life. This is what we are here for.

Life was meant to be a struggle, and it is — for everyone.

Why Suffering?

Struggle may be necessary for the purpose of life — that we participate in our creation — but why suffering? Why pain onto agony? Especially when we consider that pain is often felt by innocents, for reasons that have nothing to do with decisions they have made or something they can stop.

The reason is this: Since life in this world prepares us for life with God, life in this world must be in some way like life with God; otherwise how could our experience here prepare us to see God? Thus, when it is heading in the right direction, it is experienced as good. When it is headed in the wrong direction, it is experienced as bad — sometimes very bad.

In other words, if bad things did not hurt, good things would not be giving us a glimpse of heaven.

And if some things were not monstrous, we could not know how wonderful is the good, and how great that we achieved it.

Having Faith

The Greater the Burden, the Greater the Opportunity

It is axiomatic: Life isn't fair.

Certainly it doesn't seem fair. Its breaks and burdens are not distributed evenly.

Of course, this suggests that a good life is an easy one, that the purpose of life is a good time.

But faith says that the purpose of life is to prepare for eternal life, something we do by growing in faith and love as best we can. This we do by having faith and loving, by accepting our burdens in the name of faith and by accepting the burdens of others in the name of love.

In this view, burdens become opportunities. They become opportunities to grow in the faith and love for which we are here.

And the greater the burden, the greater the opportunity. It is here that the fairness in life is to be found.

When Someone We Love Dies...

When someone we love dies, there are eight things to remember:

1. *Those who have died are not dead*. Those who have died have gone to God to begin the life that they were made for. They are more alive than we are.

2. *If you have something to say, say it*. Those who have died have gone to God. They share His point of view. They know what is happening here on earth.

3. *The presence of our loved ones in God can color our experience of God*. Look for it. If you see it, you become more sure that your loved ones are safe. God becomes more familiar.

4. *We will see them again*. When we die. Furthermore, we will not just "see" them, we will be closer to them than we ever were on earth. Since all of us will have been transformed, we will love better. And we will never be parted again.

5. *The death of a loved one is yet another reason to let go*. Of life here. After all, now we know that life here will never be all we always hoped for. Now we know our hope is heaven. And the less attached we are to life here, the freer we feel.

6. *Grief is good*. Not the lack of faith, grief is a most natural reaction to loss. Loss, however temporary, hurts. Like the yell that vents the pain of a broken bone, grief is that internal yell that vents the pain of loss.

7. *Getting over it takes time*. To fill the space left by a human being, possibly a life companion, takes time.

Once reality without the other person sets in, it really hurts. Thereafter, there will be many ups and downs. We should not expect to see the end of the tunnel for a year and a day.

8. *Getting over it isn't bad.* Some people resist getting over grief because they feel that to do so is to betray the person who is gone. On the contrary, getting over it comes with the end of shock, the rebuilding of routine, and the gain of faith. When finally we are reunited, we will find that no love was lost. (Isn't this what we find whenever friends are reunited?)

And we will be reunited. We will.

Those who lose a loved one are often left alone. Others avoid them because they feel powerless to make things better. The truth is: Others can make things better. They can let a person talk about it. They can help a person think about something else. They can help to fill the void.

We Are Never Alone

We are never alone, least of all when we are suffering.

God suffers with us.

After all, God knows our thoughts better than we do. He knows our feelings for all that they are. Think about what this means. To know our feelings "for all that they are," one has to experience them. On account of His love for us, God can do no less. This is the price He pays to share His life with us.

This is something we need to know. Because it's true. And because it helps.

When we are suffering, it helps just to tell someone. It helps more if such a person appears to care. It helps most if we believe that our friend is just as upset as we are. Now we know we are not alone; and we will not be left alone. Now, with two carrying our burden, it weighs half as much, or even less.

God suffers with anyone whom we hurt. This we also need to know.

God Frees Us from Having to Do Everything So We Can Do Something

Question: If you believe that everything that happens follows God's plan, why bother?

Notably, this is never the attitude of those who do believe that everything that happens follows God's plan. Such people know that their lives too have followed God's plan; they love themselves, and this always inspires in them a sincere love for others.

Besides, God's plan may bring about the best thing that can happen, but it does not work apart from what we do. And until we act, and things have happened that cannot be changed, the future is ours to make. Therefore, our job is to try to see things as they are and to work for what we think is best.

Nonetheless, even though the future is ours to make, even though we can make things better or worse, we cannot spoil God's plan. Once we have acted, once something has happened that cannot be changed, whatever happened had to happen — at least for then.

God would not have put us in a position to spoil His plan. He would not have left eternity entirely in our hands.

He gives us the opportunity to make an eternal difference without giving us the unlivable burden of believing that we could make an eternal mistake.

God frees us from having to do everything so we can do something.

Two more reasons that faith in God's plan does not call for complacency:

We cannot outguess God. We do not know why His plan calls for what it does. The fact that it is raining does not necessarily mean that God does not want us to go on a picnic. Maybe He wants us to go and get wet.

We are here to grow. The fact that we did something does not mean that God wants us to continue doing it. Maybe He wants us to learn from our mistake and try harder to do better.

You Only Need to Do Your Best

You only need to do your best, the best you can as one person, the one person you actually *are*, the best you can right now. Even if your best was lousy, it was at that moment your best. You could do no more. God expects no more. He needs no more from you.

Now this does not mean that we should be satisfied with failure. After all, to do our best is to strive for success. It is to learn from our mistakes and try again. It is to evaluate what we are doing to see if it is working, and to try to think of something else if it is not. To do our best is to try to do better.

Nonetheless, at any given moment, we only need to do our best.

To know if you have done your best, you can ask yourself if you have tried.

To know if you have tried, you can ask yourself what — realistically — you could have done but didn't.

Having Faith

And to know what realistically you could have done, you can ask yourself what others do in similar situations, especially if they have similar resources and have been doing the job for a similar length of time.

✠

You only need to do your best, the best you can right now. But often it is difficult to know what the best thing is. In such a case, the principle extends to the process of making a decision: You only need to do your best, the best you can right now.

✠

You only need to do your best, the best you can right now. You are not responsible for results.

Give It Back to God

All too often we encounter a problem we cannot solve, someone's sickness we cannot cure, something broken we cannot fix.

Perhaps we tried for a long, long time.

Perhaps someone doesn't want our help, or will not hear the truth.

Perhaps the problem was ages in the making and it cannot be solved in much less time.

Perhaps the problem is not the kind that could ever be solved by *us*, or anyone like us.

In any case, we've done all that we could do. Now what?

We give it back to God.

With all reverence we say: "I've done all I could. You made it. If You want it fixed, You fix it. Of course, I'll continue to do what I can. I'll be open to the possibility that there will be an opportunity to do more. But that is up to You. In any case, I know that You know best. I know that in the end all will be well. I know that I am not God — and do not have to be."

If we can say this, we have turned our helplessness into an act of faith and the problem has already had one good effect.

But What About "Ask and You Shall Receive"?

"Ask and you shall receive." Actually, this is not true. The truth is better. We receive what we need. And God knows better than we do what we need.

Still, we need to pray. Sometimes we need to pray *for* something. But we do not pray in order to change God's mind. We pray because, to have a relationship with God, we need to be able to tell Him how we feel.

To have a relationship with anyone, we need to tell this person how we feel. If something is on our mind and we do not express it, we fail to connect. But if we do express it, even if it has nothing to do with our friend, we feel more connected than ever.

This is the reason to pray, even to pray for something. To feel connected. To know that God is there. To know that God is God, and, according to His plan, everything will be all right.

This is the reason to pray, even to pray for something. We need to express to God what we feel. But then we say: "But *Thy* will be done."

"Please, God; but *Thy* will be done."

Don't Forget to Listen

Sometimes people talk to God too much. They think that *praying* means "asking" or at the very least "telling." Prayer, however, is also listening.

To listen, we need to be quiet.

This means we need to have quiet, to make ourselves comfortable, and try our best to be relaxed. (Give it at least a minute.)

Now we simply, humbly ask God to tell us what we need to hear.

Soon a thought will begin to take shape. This is something we must let happen; it is not something we can make happen.

Often we will recognize the thought that is taking shape. Perhaps it is a thought that has been in the background and now is coming to the surface. Perhaps it is something new and different, and also a surprise.

In any case, this, the voice of our truest, deepest self, and also of God who made us in His image, is always what we need to hear.

Perhaps there is something we need to let go.

Perhaps we need to accept the love we never had to earn.

Perhaps we need to wake up to what we were doing and why.

Perhaps we need to dedicate ourselves anew.

Perhaps there is something we just need to see.

Whatever it is, it is always what we need to hear. It is also what we need to heed.

The Best Reason to Pray

The best reason to pray is this: When you pray, eventually you feel heard.

There and then you will have gained more than anything you could have prayed for. After all, if you feel heard, you know that God is listening. If you know that God is listening, you know that God is there. You know that God is God. You know that God is good. Knowing that God is good, you know that He made you not for death but for life, life with Him in heaven. Knowing that God is good, you know that He loves you, and you need only to love Him back. Finally, knowing that God is good, you know that He has a good reason for anything that happens, that He is using everything that happens to help you to prepare for life with Him.

✣

The best reason to be quiet: In silence you realize you are not alone.

What Is a Personal Relationship with God?

"I have," some say, "a personal relationship with God. It is the center of my life." What could this mean?

Faith, rightfully, originates in our deepest experiences, reflections, and judgments. It is present in anyone who has come to know that God exists. Faith becomes personal when a person's experience of God becomes an experience not only that God exists but also that He loves, that "God loves me," that "God is loving me right now."

If this becomes people's experience of God, their life of faith is not so much a life in accord with belief but rather a life inspired by love. Their experience of God gives them ongoing encouragement and guidance. Their lives have become an ongoing attempt to love God back.

The bottom line: Our faith is a personal relationship with God if only we realize that our deepest reflections put us in touch not with a thing but with a person.

We Judge God Backwards

We judge God backwards. When we hear that God loves us, we think that He loves us despite us, despite the people we really are.

Most of us are not happy with who we are. Why? Actually, there are several reasons:

We judge ourselves backwards. We get down on ourselves because we are not yet perfect rather than being happy about how far we have already come.

All of us were raised by constantly being corrected. This, of course, was necessary. Babies have to be told if they are too close to something hot or something they could break, and being corrected is how we learn to speak. But if correction was all we ever heard, it seemed that we were always wrong.

We compare our insides with other people's outsides. In other words, we are all too aware of our own imperfection. What we do not see is the inner struggle of others.

We compare ourselves to other people's things, things they have or do. We feel bad because our neighbor has a better car, as if a car says anything about the person who bought it. We feel bad because our neighbor is better at something than we are, as if any ability is more important than who we are as people, as if anything is more important than *what* we are as persons.

We compare ourselves with the people we see on television. It does not occur to us that what we see has been carefully staged to make the people we see look good. We even compare ourselves with fictional characters whose abilities or adventures are really had by no one. (Who has a new adventure every week?)

We make no allowances. We rarely take into consideration differences in ability or opportunity which none of us brought upon ourselves. (Considering how little some people were given, it's amazing how far they've come.)

The final reason that most of us are not happy with who we are is the fact that everyone else has the same problem. Thus, we are surrounded by people who have difficulty acknowledging the goodness in others and act as if there's none to see.

Not happy with who we are, most of us are not much consoled by the idea that God loves us. It says something good about God but not about us. Indeed, the idea that God loves us despite us might actually make things worse.

But God does not love us despite who we are. You cannot love what is not lovable. (You cannot love a chair.) You can only love what calls for love — what in your eyes is beautiful and good.

God loves us because of us, because each of us is who we are, because each of us in His eyes is beautiful and good.

He Couldn't Love You More

God loves each of us the only way He can — with all His heart. In order to love us with all His heart, He has put all He has into the making of each and every one of us.

God can do this because He is not like us. We are only human, limited in every way. We have only so much time, energy, and money. Therefore, we must divide up what we give, and frequently we give more to one than to another. God, however, is infinite. He could put His whole self into the making of each and every one of us. We know that He did so because He is God, because He is good, and because He had no reason not to.

This means that God has put into your making just as much as He has put into the making of everyone else, and absolutely no less than He has put into the making of anyone else.

Even more importantly, it means that *God could not love you more if you were the only person He ever made.*

In a world of limited goods and services, one person's riches diminish the value of everyone else's money. (If everyone is a millionaire, no one is rich.) But heaven is not a world of limited goods and services.

God's love for others in no way diminishes the love God has for you. What God has put into the making of others in no way diminishes the value of what God has put into the making of you.

We need to believe that we are vastly valuable — and no less so than anyone else — because we are. This is what we were made to be.

We Don't Know Why God Loves Us

God loves each of us with all His heart. He has put all He has into the making of each and every one of us. This is a beautiful thought but difficult to believe. After all, it's hard to imagine how this could be true.

It will be easier to imagine once we understand that we are here to become no more than the *seed* we will be on the day we die. This is a seed that God will complete at the moment of our death and bring to the full life of heaven. Then, just as a seed gives rise to something so much more than it was, we will become so much more than we ever were on earth — much more than we can imagine.

This, however, is what God sees now. God sees the future. We do not. Therefore, we do not know why God loves us. But we will. And so will everyone else.

Another thought about seeds: Cut one open. Look inside. We do *not* see a little flower or a little tree. What we do see does not look like much at all. It is hard to know why it is there. For this, we must wait until the seed grows into the plant. This is how it is with much that is inside us. We do not know why it is there — why we went through what we went through. But we will.

One more thought about seeds: The size of the seed has nothing to do with the size of the plant. A mustard seed is almost microscopic, but it gives rise to a big and sturdy bush. Some bulbs are bigger than the flowers they become. In like manner the worldly greatness of the seed may mean nothing in terms of eternity.

Having Faith

Why Do Some Grow So Much More Than Others?

If God loves each of us with all His heart, why, according to His plan, do some grow so much more than others?

To answer this question, it is first necessary to point out that God's plan is fashioning each of us into a *seed* whose transformation will dwarf the differences between us now. This seed, the result of a unique struggle, will give life to a unique person whose place in heaven no one else can fill.

Of course, each of us already has a place in the formation of heaven that no one else can fill. God's plan for one is also His plan for others. After all, we affect one another. In the end, the sum of these effects is going to bring about the family best suited to share God's life.

We are going to share God's life as a family. In heaven, we are going to be together. There, just as happens here, especially when people love one another, the goodness of one is going to bring good into the lives of others. In heaven, this means that all of us are going to be richer for the faith and love, that is, the holiness, of each of us. We are in this together — just like in a family.

So the whole purpose of God's plan is to prepare the family best suited to share His life, giving each and every member a unique contribution to the holiness that all of us will share.

Understanding the whole purpose of God's plan helps us to understand tragedy, for example, the deaths of infants. Here are people who had little chance to grow. Nonetheless, their deaths affect many others; their deaths affect history. Therefore, as members of the family that history will produce, they will share in the holiness to which they contributed by their death.

Understanding the whole purpose of God's plan helps us to understand the lives of those countless people who came before us and, though they did not have the chance to have much faith, did pass on to us what we needed so we could do better.

Understanding the whole purpose of God's plan helps us to understand the state of things today. After all, look where we (as a family) started. See how far we have come. Note that progress takes place slowly, and never uniformly.

Finally, understanding the whole purpose of God's plan helps us to understand ourselves — that each of us has a part to play, that each of us is irreplaceable, and that each of us is utterly special in God's eyes.

How Love Grows

It is a self-fulfilling prophecy: If we believe in the goodness within us, our goodness comes out.

If we believe that we are good, we feel good. If we feel good, we do good; we love. This is how our goodness resembles God's. His goodness had to be expressed; He made us. If we feel good, we too will care about more than just ourselves.

If we care about others, we will feel better; we will do better, and we will feel better still. This is how love grows.

If we do not see the goodness in ourselves, however, we cannot afford to see the goodness in others. The goodness in others will make us feel bad about who we are. We cannot love. (We can be nice to those from whom we want something, but this is not love and it does not last. We can do good in order to feel that we are good — that we are not bad — but we will not feel good doing it.) Not loving, we will feel worse about who we are, and so it goes.

To sum it up:

Faith makes possible the love of self.

The love of self makes possible the love of others.

The love of others makes love grow.

Part Two

LIVING FAITH

The Life of Faith Is Love

The life of faith is love. In other words, to the extent that we know God, we see God, that is, we see goodness, in ourselves and others.

To the extent that we see goodness in ourselves and others, we love.

If people have no love, they also have no faith. If they say they have faith, they do not know God nearly as well as they may think.

Faith always inspires love.

The life of love is faith. In other words, if indeed people do love, they are seeing the goodness beyond themselves. This, of course, is really God, whether or not they know it.

What Is Love?

What is love? Most people don't know. They mistake loving for liking a lot.

This is certainly the way most of us speak most of the time. We say: "I like hot dogs but I love hamburgers."

"I love my car." "I love my house." But what we mean is that we like it a lot — for what it does for us. I say, "I love you," but maybe what I mean is that I want you, in my life, for what you do for me.

This is not love. In a sense it is the opposite of love. To love is to care about others *for their sake*. If this happens, it is a huge development in the heart of any person.

All of us are born utterly self-centered. Indeed, a baby not only thinks of itself as the center of the world, a baby thinks it *is* the world; babies do not distinguish between themselves and the outside world.

Only slowly do we grow into a new idea. Only slowly do we come to understand that the world out there *is* out there, and it is home for others who are worth what I can give them.

Actually, at first we just respect others, and then, if love grows, we come to care for them, not because of what they do for us but just because they *are*.

This is love. It is interest in more-than-me. It is what makes us more like God and prepares us to share God's life forever.

It is not love if we do for others with *our* goodness on our mind. It is love when we do for others with *their* goodness on our mind.

Since to love is to care for the goodness in others, it is true: Love is a choice, not a feeling.

Sin Is Selfishness

Sin is selfishness, the true opposite of love.

But what precisely is selfishness? Is it caring about no one but ourselves? Actually, it is worse.

At birth, all of us are utterly self-centered. We are interested in no more than our bodily well-being, comfort, and food.

As we grow, however, we come to see what is out there. What we see we want. The more we see, the more we want.

With still more growth, we come to see that others are people too. As we do, we come to want progressively their attention, approval, affection, and eventually their companionship.

If we continue to grow, we develop an interest in others in themselves. Actually, at first, we just respect others, but with more development we begin to care about others for their sake. In the extreme case, another's good becomes our own.

What has happened? We grew in our sight of what is good, and what is good drew us "outside" and then "out of" ourselves. Both these developments can be spoken of as love. In both cases we are talking about an interest "beyond" ourselves. This is really, in the last analysis, an interest in God, the source of all good, and what it wants is to be one with God.

✠

A baby is utterly self-centered. Indeed, a baby not only thinks of itself as the center of the world, a baby thinks it *is* the world; babies do not distinguish between themselves and the outside world. In other words, when we are born we think that we are God. The life of faith is about growing out of this idea and into the idea that God is God, that we are part of Him, and that our hope for happiness is to become more a part of Him.

✠

Sin may be selfishness, but faith is about wanting more from life, not less.

✠

We do not need to choose between heaven and happiness here. Faith is the path to happiness here, and it wants us to enjoy — but also to share, and never to live for — all the good things that the world has to offer.

✠

In short, sin is looking inward, while love is looking outward.

Sin is also shortsightedness or the inability to defer gratification.

The Golden Rule: Why It Works and How to Make It Work for You

The golden rule — "do unto others as you would have them do unto you" — works. The golden rule works because, children of the same God, we are bearers of the same nature. What we have in common is much more important than what makes us different. Therefore, we can use our experience in order to know what others will appreciate or not. If I appreciate being treated with respect, I can presume that others will like it if I treat them with respect. If I do not like it if others treat me rudely, I should not treat others rudely. If I would feel violated if someone broke into my home and stole what is mine, I should respect the property of others. If I am stranded in a storm in the middle of the night, and someone comes to help me — and is nice about it — I will see love. Likewise, others will see love if it is I who help them.

This is how to make the golden rule work for you: Imagine how you would feel if someone did it for, or to, you. Remember how you felt when someone did it for, or to, you. Remember how the other person looked to you.

The Ten Commandments

I am the Lord your God, you shall not have strange gods before me. This first commandment is really twofold: We are asked not to believe in other spiritual powers besides God, and we are asked not to see anything but God as all-important.

You shall not take the name of the Lord in vain. Another twofold commandment: We are not to use God's name when we are not talking to God, and we are not to talk dirty.

Keep holy the Sabbath. Yet another twofold commandment. On Sunday we are to come to church, and we are to avoid all unnecessary work.

Honor thy father and thy mother. And other legitimate authority. Unless said authority asks you to violate your conscience.

Thou shall not kill. Nor injure. Not even with words.

Thou shall not commit adultery. Nor otherwise lie with your body, expressing a love and commitment you do not have.

Thou shall not bear false witness. Nor otherwise lie. The world will not work unless people tell the truth.

Thou shall not steal. Nor buy what was stolen. Nor cheat. Nor vandalize.

Thou shall not covet thy neighbor's wife or husband. In other words, strive to keep your thoughts clean.

Thou shall not covet thy neighbor's goods. In other words, resist the myth "If only. . . ."

✠

Not a modern ten "commandments," the following would better be termed a modern ten "suggestions":

1. Post "A Practical Creed" (see p. 140) where you will often see it. Read it whenever you have the chance.

2. Say the Our Father every day and mean it. Be aware that when you say, "Thy kingdom come," you are acknowledging that nothing is more important than heaven, and when you say, "Thy will be done," you are acknowledging that God's plan for you always knows best.

3. Treat others as you want them to treat you. (In moments of conflict, strive to see the situation from the other person's point of view.)

4. Recognize the lack of peace as a warning — our faith is not working.

5. Strive to be honest with yourself about what you're feeling. Remember, feelings aren't shameful, but what we do about them can be.

6. Treat television as the potential addictor which it is. Watch as little as you can. Have rules and keep them. Never talk about anything just because it was on television.

7. Keep the two-hour rule, to wit: Leave yourself the last two hours of almost every day to do, or not do, as you wish.

8. Get enough sleep. Make choices for this purpose.

9. Come to church. Be as faithful to God as you want God to be faithful to you.

10. Give back to God sacrificially. And considering the amount that most of us spend on things we do not need, it is difficult to imagine that the traditional ten percent would be too much.

Greed

After substance abuse and unchastity, the sin which most often mars the lives of otherwise good people is greed.

By "greed" we are not referring to anything criminal nor even anything extraordinary. By "greed" we are referring to the attitude which says that every cent I make is mine, mine to spend on me. And if I am cornered into giving anything to charity, it will be as little as I can justify *and you're lucky to get that.*

Greed looks at things backwards. It asks, What must I give? But we are called to ask, What can I justify keeping?

To make a good decision, I must remember that charity, that is, love, shows itself only in sacrifice.

Therefore, it costs me something I wanted and could otherwise have bought. It costs me savings that could otherwise have made me feel more secure.

Love also lasts. Therefore, I give and give again. I give more often than I may be thanked. I let others count on me. (I put it in my budget — and it is not the first thing to be cut.)

Still, the love of self does come first. I am called to take care of myself and my family (as people of this century) and not to add to the burdens of others (if, for example, I should become sick or old). This is what I *need*. The rest, at least, is what I should give. And be grateful for the opportunity.

Guides for giving are helpful. They give us goals to shoot for, and they spare us from endless analysis.

"Tithing," ten percent, preferably before taxes, is often a fair measure of what a person or family can afford. Justly, those who tithe are asked to devote five percent to their community and five percent to other things deserving of their support.

In some places, people are asked to give weekly one hour's wage.

More challenging for some would be the rule "Give an amount equal to what you spend on you." Here we are talking about the money you spend going out to dinner, or on shows, sports, toys, and vacation.

Regardless of the rule we use, giving should normally attempt to cover the bases of our obligations. Here we are talking about our own community, other things that we believe in, the poor, and people in crisis.

A simple sign of sacrificial giving: We can mention various things that we would really like, that we could really afford, but did not get because of our giving.

The Corporal Works of Mercy

Feed the hungry. We should also feed the lonely, especially on holidays.

Give drink to the thirsty. Since people can almost always get water, the second corporal work of mercy really asks for generosity with one's time and willingness to converse.

Clothe the naked. Since they are spared from throwing out their perfectly good used clothing, those who donate may well receive more than those who get the donation. But this does not excuse people from their extravagance.

Give shelter to the stranger. We also give shelter to the stranger when we share the neighborhood with people who are not just like me.

Visit the sick. And the homebound. Or at least a regular call.

Minister to prisoners. And give a chance to those who have paid their debt.

Bury the dead. And call on the mourners a month after the funeral.

The Spiritual Works of Mercy

Convert sinners. This we do not do by calling them names or threatening them. We share our faith by living it, and by showing its results — peace, joy, and love.

Teach the ignorant. But it will never happen if we blame them for their ignorance.

Counsel the doubtful. Step one: Recognize the reasons for their doubts.

Console the sorrowful. But not by crying with them. This only confirms their feeling that all is lost. We also contradict our faith by seeming desperate to help.

Bear wrongs patiently. Isn't this what we expect others to do? We tell others that sins against them help them grow.

Forgive injuries. Usually what was injured was our ego. Therefore, an injury is an opportunity to believe in ourselves.

Pray for the living and the dead. If we pray for something, we teach ourselves to want it. Therefore, praying for others helps *us*.

In praying for the dead, we are asking God to do what we believe He will do, or we are thanking Him for what we believe He did do. This is the way we acknowledge that He didn't have to do it.

The Only Sure Sign of Love

Only in action do we show what we really believe. And only in sacrifice do we show that what we feel is really love. Only in sacrifice do I show that I am interested in more than just me.

There are many ways we can sacrifice: We can sacrifice our time. We can sacrifice our energy. We can sacrifice something that we would rather do.

We can sacrifice our money. The sacrifice of money is the easiest to measure. Now, this is not to say that the more one gives the better the one is — after all, the person who gives more might have more to give — but we can measure our giving against our means, the giving of others of similar means, or our spending on ourselves.

We can sacrifice our security — our desire not to be embarrassed or rejected. This is what we are doing if we try something that may not succeed, or if we offer friendship that may not be returned. This is what we are doing if we try to share our faith — or at least stand up for it.

We can sacrifice our health, our safety, or our life.

In any case, sacrifice is the only sure sign of love. We would do well to keep this in mind as we listen to others and look at ourselves.

Time will tell. Since enthusiasm is often fleeting, only in perseverance do we show what we really believe.

There Are Many Ways to Give Up Your Life

Sacrifice is the essential sign of love. In the ultimate case, it means giving up your life.

This, essentially, is what the life of faith is all about. You give your life back to God, and He will give it back to you in glory.

There are many ways to give up your life. The most obvious, of course, is martyrdom. In this case, you give up your life all at once.

But it is also possible to give up your life bit by bit, day by day. This you do in any life of service. This you do in marriage when, on account of love, you "spend" your life with another person. You give up your life when you accept in your heart that things can never be the way you always wanted.

There are many ways to give up your life.

Nothing is more wonderful than to give up your life. Yet if faith is wrong about life with God, to give up your life would be a mistake.

The More You Put Into It, the More You Appreciate It

Great things never come easy. We have to work hard and long. Things never go just as we have planned. We suffer many setbacks. We can expect opposition.

Fortunately, we are rewarded for everything we endure because the more we put into it, the more we appreciate it. This is not only the testimony of those who have endured much for their achievements, but it is also bespoken by the people's lack of appreciation for what came easy.

We have little reason to appreciate what came easy. When we look at what we have or what we have done, we see nothing to make us proud. We as persons were not involved. Neither our faith, our love, nor our strength had to come through.

Not so with what we had to work for. And the more we put into it, and the more and the longer we suffered, the more we appreciate it.

The good thing about a bad start: It helps you to appreciate that what you accomplished was not easy.

The Exercise of Faith Strengthens It

The exercise of a muscle strengthens it. We might expect the exercise of a muscle to deplete it. But, no, the exercise of a muscle strengthens it.

In like manner, the exercise, the living out, of faith strengthens it.

This happens for four reasons:

First of all, in order to live our faith, we have to think about it. We have to remind ourselves of what and why we believe.

Second, as we live out our faith, we experience the superiority of a life that only faith makes sense of.

Third, as we live out our faith, and are seen doing so, we give up what holds us back — the appeal of not taking a stand.

Finally, as we live out our faith, taking a stand at its side, we give ourselves another reason to want it to be true.

The exercise of faith strengthens it. Thus it is that the rich get richer and the poor lose the little they have.

✣

The poor lose the little they have because *not* exercising their faith, *not* doing anything differently because of their faith, they tell themselves, "Maybe it isn't true," over and over again.

This also happens when people ignore opportunities to speak of their faith, or they stand by and allow it to be contradicted.

No Good Work Is Ever Wasted

In this age of gargantuan statistics, the little we can do often seems not worth the effort. We forget that every little bit counts — a lot.

For one thing, you never know. A small kindness can make a big difference on a bad day. A simple thought can lead someone to a big insight. Maybe the person you encouraged will go on to make an even bigger difference in someone else's life.

For another thing, in loving, *you* grew.

Living Faith

Even if you did not grow much, who knows what will come from a little extra holiness when finally we die and are transformed?

Considering that the fruits of the holiness of ourselves and others will last forever, it is clear that all growth has infinite value.

Therefore, even though we are also called to be concerned about the best use of our time and energy, we can still be sure that no good work is ever wasted.

Faith Is Its Own Reward

People of faith are not immune to envy. Sometimes they are especially envious of those who do bad things and seem to get away with them.

To combat such feelings, people of faith need to realize that faith is its own reward. People of faith have so much more than anyone without it.

First of all, they know more. They know where they come from. They know why they are here. They know where they are going when they die.

People of faith know that they are not going to die. They know that they are going to live, to live with God forever. They know that they are going to have all that their hearts already desire — the only place where this can happen.

People of faith know that they are here to grow in the love that prepares them for life with God. Therefore, they have a reason to make a difference in this world, and to live the only kind of life that can make a person happy.

Finally, people of faith know that God is working with them, through everything that happens to them, to prepare them to become the people they were meant to be. Therefore, they have all the reason in the world to accept themselves for who they are, to accept their past for what it was, and to face their future without fear.

If all of this were not enough, faith is the deepest knowledge that we can have. It bespeaks the deepest person that we can be. And every experience of this deeper person is, to that extent, richer. The person with faith is more alive than anyone without it.

✤

In the face of human life at its lowest, the proper response is not indignation but gratitude.

Love Is Its Own Reward

Faith is its own reward. So is love.

This was to be expected. After all, we are here to grow in love as best we can. Therefore, we were made so that nothing else can make us happy. God would

Living Faith

not have made us so that we can be happy going in the wrong direction. Therefore, when we are selfish we are never satisfied, whereas when we love we are always happy.

With love, our happiness is in our own hands.

When we love, when we are worried about other people's problems, our own problems seem much less serious.

When we love others, others usually love us.

Finally, when we love, we are better at staying out of trouble, especially of our own making.

Love is its own reward. And the lack of love is its own punishment.

We know that we cannot live without breathing, that we can get around human nature; but some of us think that we can be happy without loving.

One does not seek fulfillment. Fulfillment is a by-product of service.

If faith is wrong about life with God, the only life that can make us happy makes no sense.

Try to See Things from Others' Point of View

It is yet another form of love. It is the only way two sides will ever come to a good agreement. It is the only way that discussion will ever make things *better*. We need to try to see things from others' point of view.

If we won't even try, how can we expect someone to try to see things from our point of view?

How do we do it? We ask ourselves: How would I have felt if I were there, if I were you, if this or that had happened to me...? If we are honest about it:

We will understand others or events better;

we may find out that we were "wrong";

and even if we still believe we were "right," we will have all the more reason to think so.

✠

People should feel themselves called to look at something from another person's point of view every time they find themselves angry at someone, or inclined to judge or disappoint someone.

Apologizing, Who Looks Bad?

Think about it. Think about those times that people have apologized to you; they said they were sorry. In doing so, did anyone ever look bad? Quite the contrary, apologizing, people look great. They look real; they look strong; they look like they care about your feelings. This is always everyone's experience of other people apologizing.

Nonetheless, many of us still have the idea that if *we* apologize, we look bad. Perhaps we're afraid that we're revealing that we're not perfect. Chances are that others already know. And, not apologizing, not being able to apologize, now we look even more imperfect.

Apologizing, we have nothing to lose — and everything to gain. We will look good. Having recognized our mistake, and what we have to work on, we will grow. Finally, acknowledging our imperfection, in other words, acknowledging that we're not God, we will no longer feel that we need to be God.

So What If I'm the Only One?

Much is not done because "I would be the only one."

It's interesting. It doesn't bother me if I am the only one who gets the prize, but when it comes to sacrifice, I cannot be the only one.

But am I not here to prepare for life with God? Am I not called to do my best, the best I can as one person, the one person I happen to be, the best I can today?

Isn't my best my share of the solution to any problem — if only everybody did it?

Isn't my love greater if I am the only one — or at least I was the first?

Besides, "everybody" will never be inspired to do it until somebody starts.

Love Surpasses Justice

A baby at birth is utterly self-centered. The baby does not recognize that others even exist.

As we grow, however, we come to recognize that not only do others exist but they are people just like us.

Now we give others respect, respecting their persons, their property, their right to hear the truth. This is the level of justice. It gets its name from the idea that doing good deserves its reward while being bad deserves its punishment. Also involved is the idea that by their actions people make themselves good or bad, an idea which is called self-righteousness.

If we continue to grow, however, we come to see that others are good in themselves, good just because they are people, so good that they are worth what we can give them regardless of what they have done, even if they have hurt us. This is called love.

As we can see, love surpasses justice.

God Does Not Keep Score

God does not keep score. He does not see us as our record, our PERMANENT RECORD, of the bad things we have done.

God sees us as *persons* who can learn, and when we do we turn a bad thing we did into a good thing we now know or now know better.

This is our power to turn bad into good. We can use it any time. We can use it all the time. No matter what we did. No matter how long we did it. Once we recognize that it was wrong, we convert it from a bad thing that we did into a good thing that is in us. We are more, not less, because of what has happened.

Indeed, learning from things especially wrong can bring about growth especially great. We grow more than we would ever have otherwise. This is the reason that people are often able to say: "It was bad, but I'm glad it happened."

In any case, God does not look at us for what we did. He looks at us for who we are.

One obstacle to putting the past behind us is the hurt we might have caused others, many of whom may still be hurting. How can we feel good about what we have learned if it came at such a price?

We remind ourselves that just as it was good for *us* to struggle with something hard, and to grow by doing so, this is no less true for others. By causing trouble, we have given others an opportunity to grow.

In the case of mothers, fathers, and friends, we have given them an opportunity to love in a very special way. After all, when we are good to others, love for us is easy. In the case of strangers, we have given them an opportunity for faith.

That others may not have chosen to accept these opportunities was ultimately their decision. As long as we have done all we could to help them — apologizing and otherwise making amends — we can go in peace.

How We Will See Our Sins

To get to heaven, we will need to be transformed. Once we are transformed, we will look back at our sins and we will understand — why we did what we did, why we were unable to do better, and all the good God brought out of it. Best of all, from our point of view in heaven, our sins will bother us even less than we are bothered now by the mistakes we made when we were children.

When we were little children, we made many mistakes; we did many silly things. We know it, but it doesn't bother us. It may have bothered us at the time but it doesn't bother us now. We could see it all on video, but it wouldn't — at least it shouldn't — embarrass us.

What is more, the difference between us as children and us as adults will be nothing compared with the difference between us here and us in heaven.

Parents understand their children's mistakes. They look at their children's struggles with love. And when their children finally learn, they are only overjoyed.

God understands His children's mistakes. He looks at His children's struggles with love. And when His children finally learn, He is only overjoyed.

We Are All Far from the Kingdom of God

We cannot know what we will be in heaven. But this much we can know: From the point of view of heaven, the differences between us here are no big deal.

Here we see a big difference between saints and sinners. From the point of view of heaven, no one here is nearly perfect — and all of us are trying.

Here we see a big difference between rich and poor. From the point of view of heaven, all of us are terribly poor, powerless, and in need.

Here we see a big difference between those we call happy and those we call sad. From the point of view of heaven, all of us have a horrible life.

The fact is: *We are all far from the kingdom of God.* Keeping this in mind makes us less conceited and more open to grow. It makes us more compassionate with those who might be just a bit behind us. And, if we perceive ourselves as the ones behind, it will make us less envious.

How "Judge Not, or You Will Be Judged" Really Works

The injunction "Judge not, or you will be judged" seems simple enough. Do not judge others, or God will judge you. Actually, God need not be bothered. If you judge others, you will judge yourself for Him.

We start judging, that is, we are critical, because of insecurity. Not feeling terribly good about ourselves, we are tempted by the idea that we can feel better by seeming to be better than other people. Thus we criticize. In an imperfect world, we can always find something to criticize.

This, however, does not work.

First of all, deep down, we know what we are doing. This makes us feel only worse about ourselves.

Second, by constant criticism, our idea of what a human has to be becomes harder and harder to satisfy. Eventually this idea comes back to bite us; this gives us all the more need to criticize... and the cycle starts again.

But we can reverse the cycle. Instead of practicing criticism, we can practice compassion.

We start by calling to mind the truth of our faith which says that we were made good, that we never choose what is bad because it is bad, that we do our best with what we were given.

We see this in ourselves.

Then we vindicate this truth by seeing it in others.

If we can do this, we will feel less need to criticize; our compassion will come more easily... and a new cycle will have started.

People speak of the faults of others in order to feel better about themselves. Once they realize this, it no longer works.

Compassion for self based on compassion for others might seem an excuse for sin. Such might be so if compassion for self *were* an excuse for sin — a reason to keep on sinning. But this is never the experience of compassionate people. Such people love themselves;

they believe in themselves, and they need to do their best. Since they are at peace with themselves, they are more aware of what they are doing and why, and what they need to do in order to do better.

✣

Compassion for others must come first. We cannot accept in ourselves what we would not accept in others.

Forgiveness Is Understanding

Forgiveness is understanding.

First of all, forgiveness is understanding that no one is perfect, that all of us are born imperfect — unformed, unknowing, and utterly self-centered — and we can grow only so far.

Forgiveness is understanding that none of us had the benefit of perfect parenting, or was completely spared from confusing or damaging experiences.

Forgiveness is understanding that some of us received no parenting, or were the victims of horribly confusing and damaging experiences.

Of course, forgiveness is also understanding that, deep down, what we really want is good. We never choose what is bad because it is bad. People choose what is bad because, from their point of view, this is what they have to do to survive, to be somebody, or even to be loved — and they know no better.

In sum, forgiveness is understanding that people do the best they can with what they are given. This must be true if God is good and made us good.

But, though God made us good, we still begin life as babies. We are born utterly selfish, and ever afterwards our selfishness is often on display. This, of course, is sin. It is not good. It is unbeautiful. It is the opposite of Godly.

Thus, we *are* allowed to hate the sin, but we are called to understand the sinner.

People may be foolish, but they are never fools.

I am arrogant to insist that there is no goodness deep down within a person because I cannot see it.

Forgiveness Is the Decision Not to Hate

Forgiveness is understanding that people do the best they can with what they are given. Forgiveness is understanding that he who hurt us is not evil. In essence, forgiveness is the decision not to hate.

But this does not mean that now we like him.

It does not mean that now we trust him. Not if there is no sign he has changed. (Though forgiveness does mean that we are open to the possibility.)

✣

When we hate, we're the ones who suffer.

Forgiveness Is a Vote of Confidence in Self

The hardest things to forgive are those offenses that struck at our soul, our sense of ourselves. They were those times we were treated as though we were worthless, those actions that took from us something that in our mind gave us value, those words that confirmed our worst fears about ourselves.

In such cases, forgiveness is not about accepting someone else's humanity. It is much harder; it is about accepting our own humanity. It is about accepting God's design of us rather than our own. It is about believing in ourselves by virtue of our own decision and not because of the opinion of any other person.

It is a vote of confidence in self.

Sometimes to see it this way is the only thing that can get us past our pain.

People Have the Power Over You You Give Them

People agonize over the opinions of others. In order not to do so:

Think about the people you depend on. You don't worry about what they are thinking. You know what they are thinking — for well or for ill — and you live with it just fine.

So who do we worry about? Often they are not even people whom we know. They are people we may never see again. They are people whose opinion we do not respect with regard to any other matter. They are people who do nothing for us, or who are not in a position to do less.

So what are we afraid of? What power do these people have over us?

In fact, they have no power over us except the power we give them — seeking what may be their passing or misplaced admiration.

And we may not even get it. After all, others have their own reasons to see things one way or another. Some people will hate you if only because everyone else likes you. Some people will speak ill of you if only because you are trying so hard to get no one to speak ill of you. What is worse, one mistake — or someone's vicious lie — and people will never look at us the same.

We cannot assure ourselves of people's admiration. Therefore, we do not need to try. We do better to remember that He who knows us best loves us best, and is preparing us to become who others will see and love in heaven. We do better to remember that the only power people have over us is the power we give them trying to win their admiration. Therefore, once we say it doesn't matter, it doesn't.

Ironically, once we have decided that we do not care what others think, we always impress them.

Who has more to be proud of: those who are everything everyone expects, or those who are happy being themselves?

Fifty thousand years from now, who will know the difference?

Once the news is old, who but you will care?

Once you are gone, what will *you* care?

You are the only person who cares that you're not perfect. (You are the only person who ever thought you might be perfect.)

The Charity of Friendship and Love of Family

In its insistence on a love of enemies and strangers, faith can give the impression that there is something less noble in a love of those we know and like. After all, this is a love that pays us back.

True enough. But the love of enemies and strangers is often easy. To love an enemy, all we have to do is say, "Forget it." To love a stranger, all we have to do is write a check. Normally, we do not need to give much of our time, and rarely do we need to give much of ourselves.

This is not the case with the love of friends or family. This is love that must be lived out, day after day, with no end in sight.

It is a love that must do much more than another person could ever thank you for.

It is a love not built on courtesy or pretense.

Indeed, it is a love that has to endure many bad days.

It is a love that cares for another person for the best possible reason: You are the specific and special person you are, and not someone else.

Hence the greatness, that is, the charity, of friendship and love of family.

Which is better, to love personally those who love you, or to love at a distance those who do nothing for you?

The answer: Neither is necessarily better. The two loves exercise different aspects of our spirit. And, as with exercise of our body, if you exercise only one muscle, the body suffers.

How Many People Can Hold Your Hand?

People thrive on the support of others, and the more the better.

But the support we need is best measured in terms of "personal" support — the support of people whom we know, with whom we share our lives, who know how hard we're trying... people we admire, who admire us for us, in a whole-hearted way, and have dedicated at least a part of their lives to supporting us. Since they will need something similar from us, this is something we can receive only from a few. Nonetheless, it is the best the world can do in terms of support. Such support is worth much more than the distant, "soft" support that some people receive from various forms of fame.

It is better to have one friend than a million fans.

Living Faith

The Religion in Romance

As of love of someone we enjoy loving, who so wonderfully loves us back, romance would seem the least holy love of all. Not so.

What is love? Love is what happens when we see the good beyond ourselves. First, we respect who we see. Then, we desire to care for whom we see. Ultimately, we desire to be one with whom we see.

Such is being "in" love. Not only do we desire to share our whole life, indeed our whole self, with another person; the other's good has become our own. To the extent possible here on earth, we are one.

In heaven, we will be one with God and with one another. Thus, romance presents the true goal of love better than any other form of love. It is the best result of seeing the goodness, of seeing God, in one of the creatures who were made to make Him known.

There *is* religion in romance.

We might suspect that romance will cause two people to become interested in one another to the exclusion of all else. In fact, the contrary is true. In the security and joy that two people can give to one another, they are freed and inspired to see the good in others.

We Want Our Feelings to Be Returned

It is a fundamental fact of human nature: We want our feelings to be returned.

If we respect someone, we want this person to respect us. If he or she does not, we feel bad.

If we like someone, we want this person to like us. If he or she does not, we feel worse.

If we fall in love with someone, we want this person to fall in love with us. If he or she does not, we are devastated.

Of course, even if the object of our affection appears in love with us, our troubles are far from over. After all, if we fall in love — and what we feel is really love — it means that we have come to see another person as someone very special, someone very good. For all intents and purposes, we adore this other person. But we want our feelings to be returned. Therefore, we need this person to adore us.

All of this makes us very *sensitive* to those we love, sensitive to anything they say or do that we in any way take to be a criticism, sensitive to any indication that they might be more impressed with anyone else, in any way, at any time.

We need to know this so that we will not be quick to blame the other person for our pain. It is much like having a sore. If we have a sore, and someone (accidentally) touches it, we are hurt, not because the other person was so bad, but because love has made us sensitive.

We also need to remember that the other person feels exactly the same way. We need to handle him or her with care. In particular, we must strive never to speak to the other person in a way that we would never want him or her to speak to us.

We want our feelings to be returned. We really do.

The Difference Between Enjoyment and Idolatry

Made by God, things are good. Indeed, in creating, God drew upon Himself. Therefore, in created things, we get a glimpse of God.

We can see God in the beauty and complexity of nature, in the mountains and the seas, in plants, animals, and us.

We can see God in our own handiwork, in art and in science, which explore creation and reveal the hand of the Creator.

We can experience God in all kinds of good times, as we experience the richness of what creation can be, and we get a glimpse of what life with God will be.

Creation is good. It is to be enjoyed.

But is not to be adored.

Creation is not our hope, and nothing in creation is of ultimate importance — something that I have to have no matter what.

To see anything of this world as of ultimate importance is idolatry. It is wrong.

Idolatry is wrong, first of all, because it is incorrect. It is to seek our salvation in something that cannot save.

Idolatry is also wrong because it is to seek our happiness in something that cannot make us happy.

Finally, idolatry is wrong because it causes us to do wrong in order to get or to keep things. When finally we are trapped or caught, then it causes suffering.

The Difference Between Needs and Desires

Because we are not God, we have needs that must be met.

But there is a problem. Needs look just like other desires — including our desires for things we should not have. Therefore, how do we know which of our desires are really needs?

The answer is contained in the old observation "Some people eat to live, others live to eat."

In the first case, the people desire food so that they will be sustained to go about the business of their lives.

Indeed, taking care of this *need* for food is a big part of the joy of eating.

As it turns out, people need various things so that they will be sustained — also in spirit — to go about the business of their lives.

Therefore, to know the difference between needs and desires, we ask simply: Do we want it to live — for the sake of being sustained to do what really matters to us — or do we live to have it? We might also ask Does it take more than it gives?

It Is Balance That Gives Joy

Joy does *not* come because we always have the best of everything. If we always have the best of everything, we get tired of it, no matter what it is. We need to look for more and more. This will lead to self-destruction. Joy comes when things are special — when we do not have them all the time.

Joy comes from balance — the balance between work and play, work and rest, staying home and going out, Christmas and the rest of the year.... The joy in life comes from going back and forth.

You work hard. You go out to dinner. You talk about what you do. You give it meaning. You go back to work. This way you can enjoy your next night out.

It is balance that gives joy. And, as it turns out, since balance involves the basics, joy is available to everyone.

The Ingredients of a Great Life

It is yet another bad effect of television. Since people watch so much television, and "stars" are all that people see, stars are all that people want to be. Anything else is just a life.

This is a mistake for several reasons.

First of all, stardom and greatness are hardly synonymous.

Stardom and happiness are rarely synonymous.

Furthermore, stardom is rarely in our own hands. In almost every case, people need a break; they need to "know" someone; they need to be lucky enough to have a good day on the right day. Stardom is not something people can bring about solely by their own talent and determination.

Finally, stardom is available only to a few. If everyone is famous (or rich), no one is famous (or rich). But what would this say about God? Is it possible that God made life in such a way that only a few of His children can have a great one?

Doesn't it make more sense to suppose that God made a great life available to everyone? This is precisely what we will see as we investigate the true ingredients of a great life.

To begin with, we should expect that a great life would have something to do with the purpose of life. The purpose of life is to prepare for life with God. We do this through a life of faith. Since this is what life is for, we should suppose that God made us so that we will be most happy when this is what we are doing. And so we are.

Of course, living faith also means being responsible for ourselves and those we love. This means work. A work is good if it provides people with the good things that they need. A good work actually contributes to *everyone's* life and growth. After all, life in modern society requires many people to do their job. Work further exercises our faith if we do our best — if we do our job with pride — and if we treat the public honestly and kindly. Work is satisfying if it allows us to pursue some of our natural interests and to exercise some of our natural talents.

But a great life may also involve an "avocation." An avocation is something we do for enjoyment or enrichment — but not as our work. How sad it is when people quit playing or painting or some other activity *which they say they enjoy* solely because no one will pay them to do it.

A great life also involves leisure. This is time we spend in conversation (especially at meals), at prayer, and in simple reflection. It is here that we live best because it is here that we experience our life.

Of course, a great life also involves relationships — the making and keeping of friendships. A source of joy, a way to love, friendship is an indispensable ingredient of a great life.

Most people marry. Marriage provides companionship, this world's greatest gift. Marriage is also an opportunity to love as God loves us — to love another person because of who that person is. This makes marriage both a great life and way to greatness at the same time.

The same can be said of having children. A source of countless joys, being a parent is also a lot of work and the most important work there is. Think about it. If one could cure cancer, the best result would be that people would live a little longer (maybe) so that they would grow a little holier (maybe). But being a parent is direct cooperation with God in the creation and formation of the family which we will be forever. What could be greater than that?

A great life is available to everyone who knows what greatness is.

Part Three

PRACTICING FAITH

Practicing Faith

We Were Made to Be a Family

Essentially, the faith of the Church is faith in the Church. In other words, it is faith that we who are going to be family in heaven are called to be a family here on earth.

We are going to be a family in heaven. In heaven, we are going to be together. There, just as happens here, especially when people love one another, the goodness of one is going to bring good into the lives of others. In heaven, the goodness of one is going to bring good into the lives of all others.

We can picture this in terms of light. In heaven, each of us will shine according to our holiness, our likeness to God. But the light from each of us will give more light to all. Thus, all of us are going to be richer for the holiness of each of us.

Therefore, it is clear, ours is a common destiny. Thus did God make us such that our lives are richer in every way when they are shared. Our faith is stronger when we share it. We are stronger when we are united. For this reason, we are called to be a Church, one Church, one family in faith. This is the belief *we were made to be a family*.

Why We Look Up

The proof of this idea is its explanation. The fact is: Our lives mean nothing unless they are shared. This is a fact of life *so* fundamental that we sometimes overlook it. Nonetheless, it *is* a fundamental fact of life, and it tells about how we are supposed to live our faith and how we are going to live in heaven.

Actually, the belief *we were made to be a family* pulls together and helps us to understand all our other basic beliefs.

It tells us a lot about what heaven will be, assuring us that we will be together with the people whom we love.

It shows us that love is smart in every way. After all, not only are all others people we will love as brothers and sisters, but also we are all going to be richer for everyone we help to grow. Besides this, it makes sense of self-sacrifice, something that otherwise makes no sense.

Finally, it helps us to see the wisdom of God's plan, something that is not always obvious person by person. After all, the whole purpose of God's plan is the creation of our family. Sometimes He asks some to have less so that in the end all will have more.

But why were we made to be a family? We were made to be a family because God is a family, the family we refer to as the Father, the son, and the holy spirit.

What this means is actually quite simple. Everything comes from God. This means that first everything had to exist "in" God. But what about the many things that can exist only if there is more than one of us involved — friendship, romance, teamwork, and everything else that would never have existed if God had made only one person? It cannot be that these things were new to God when first they existed on earth. They must have existed in God already. Obviously, God is more than one person as we are persons; He is more than any one of us can know on our own. This is the reason that to share His life most fully He made us to be a family. And how did He make us to be a family? The holiness that lets us see God is the product of the life, work, suffering, and death of us all inseparably.

The Glory Be

Glory be to the Father, and to the son, and to the holy spirit. As it was in the beginning, is now, and will be forever. Amen.

In other words: Dear God, I realize that Yours is the life of a family, and that we Your children are called to be a family too.

The Role of Christ in Christian Faith

Jesus was sent to point out to us the truth that was written into all of our hearts, and to call us to become the one family in faith that we were meant to be.

The Father had to send us someone.

No one on his own has the right to speak for God. Therefore, to call us to become one family in faith, God had to send someone to speak in His name.

This was the mission of Jesus of Nazareth, "the son of God." Born of Mary some two thousand years ago, Jesus was the son sent to teach us that we too are God's children.

Jesus founded the Church by calling together "disciples." From among them he named the "apostles" to be their leaders. He named Peter to be the leader of the apostles.

Jesus' teaching brought him into conflict with the religious leaders of his day. Jealous of their power, and especially so when Jesus came to Jerusalem, their capital, they plotted to have him killed by the Romans who ruled their country. They told the Romans that Jesus was trying to overthrow them and establish a worldly kingdom. Wanting no trouble, the Romans arrested Jesus; this happened on a Thursday, immediately after Jesus' last supper with the apostles. The next day Jesus was crucified, died, and was buried.

Jesus accepted the cross in order to demonstrate the faith and love to which all of us are called. He accepted the cross in order to demonstrate that sacrifice is the supreme sign of love.

The cross was also meant to demonstrate God's love for us. In sending His son to give up his life, God could do no more to show His love. He did this to show us that He could not love us more. He could not love us more because He has put His whole self into our making.

On Sunday, Jesus began to appear to the apostles. This — the resurrection — was the supreme sign that Jesus was in a special way God's son. We know that Jesus rose because, if he did not, we would have no reason to be his followers and humanity would not be able to become one family in faith.

Five Reasons We Believe That Jesus Rose

Of course, the cross makes no sense without the resurrection. But this raises the question, How do we know that Jesus rose? Historical testimony is one thing, but historical testimony can be mistaken. People sometimes make up stories or simply believe what they want to. They may even die for such stories. This is what Christians say in *not* accepting as true the fantastic stories of other people's religions. What makes ours more believable?

Actually, there are *five* reasons we believe in the resurrection:

1. *We already agree with Jesus.* The truth of Christian doctrine was written into our hearts. Indeed, Christian doctrine makes sense to everyone regardless of race, age, education, or background. Clearly, the human spirit was made to receive its gifts.

2. *It rings true.* The idea that Jesus would appear to his followers after his self-sacrificial death seems the best way God could confirm what Jesus taught — that we were made for life immortal, and that faith and love are the way we get there.

3. *The record is credible.* The earliest testimonies to the resurrection — most notably Paul's first letter to the Corinthians — were written during Christianity's first generation. Furthermore, it is clear that the resurrection was central to the first Christians' faith. Although it is also clear that the stories were written to make certain points, these points bespeak the underlying conviction that Jesus rose. Finally, it is evident that the resurrection stories were based on the experiences of several people, none of whom seem to have profited from whatever authority the experience may have given them.

4. *It explains Christianity.* By the first Christians' own admission, when Jesus was arrested, they fled.

Practicing Faith

Yet after Jesus' death, they went on to preach his teachings throughout the Roman Empire. This was especially remarkable when we consider that Jesus' first followers were people of no stature in the empire. This notwithstanding, the communities they founded went on to become the world's dominant faith. Surviving the death of its charismatic founder, this faith cannot be explained as a cult. Furthermore, the Scriptures give no evidence of the kinds of techniques which cult leaders use in order to maintain control of their followers.

5. Most of all, we believe in the resurrection because *we need it*. If Jesus did not rise, we would have no reason to be his followers and humanity would not be able to become one family in faith. In other words, we know that Jesus rose because everything else we know to be true depends on it. If the apostles did not have a real experience of Jesus as alive — if they either imagined or made it up — Christianity was founded on a falsehood. Even more importantly, we would have no reason to insist that Jesus was God's son, sent to found His Church.

Though the principal evidence of the resurrection is the fact that we need it, the resurrection story would not serve us were it not historically plausible. Therefore, the evidence of the resurrection is like the two sides of a pitched roof. They hold each other up.

The Six Symbolisms of the Candle

Think about it. If we read the story of Jesus' crucifixion, we get a fairly clear picture of what actually happened. But what about Jesus' resurrection? Did Jesus just wake up in the tomb? It doesn't say. Did his body just disappear and then appear somewhere else? It doesn't say. Who moved the stone? What actually happened? The truth is: We do not know. Therefore, the official symbol of the resurrection is a lighted candle, an abstract symbol, one which helps us to understand what we do know — that sometime after his death Jesus shined into the lives of his chosen disciples to let them know that he was alive with God the Father.

Not just an abstract symbol of the resurrection, candlelight is also a symbol of faith per se, the truth that lets us see differently and live a better life. When we know that we were made for life with God, we see the things we have — and don't have — differently. When we know that we are here to prepare for life with God, which we do by faith and love, we feel differently when we need faith or love. And when we know that God works with us, through everything He sends into our lives, we can take what happens — and our lives and ourselves — so very differently.

Practicing Faith

The flame is also a great symbol of faith because it moves; it looks alive. In this, it is a wonderful reminder that faith gives life; it gives peace, purpose, and joy. The person with faith is more alive than anyone without it.

The lighting of one candle from another is a wonderful symbol of the way we can give our faith to others and still keep it. This symbol is especially appropriate because it helps us to picture the way one person's faith can light the candle of many others, each of whom can light the faith of many others. . . .

But if we fail to share our faith. . . . The flame is also a symbol of faith because if you cover it you kill it. To cover faith diminishes it because when we fail to speak of our faith or we keep quiet when it is contradicted, we tell ourselves "maybe it isn't true" over and over again.

When faith *is* shared. . . . Picture a dark room filled with people holding unlit candles. Someone enters with a light. This person proceeds to light the candles of those he meets and they in turn light the candles of those near them. Soon the room is filled with much light and everyone will share it. This includes the person who entered with the light. He sees much better than if he had failed to share his light.

The Cross and the Basics

The cross is simultaneously a statement of faith in all three basics.

The cross is a statement of faith in heaven because, on the cross, Jesus gave up his life here.

The cross is a statement of faith in love because sacrifice is love.

Finally, the cross is a statement of faith in God's plan because it would not have happened unless Jesus chose to accept it.

The Four Meanings of the Cross

The following are four meanings of the cross:

1. *To bear a cross is the road to glory.* It is certainly the road of faith and love. It is the road of faith because a cross is bearable only if we really believe that God knows what He is doing in giving it to us. It is the road of love because it is sacrifice; it is the sacrifice of our life, our lifetime, or our dreams.

2. *God could not love us more.* In becoming one of us and giving up His life for us, God could do no more to show His love. This showed that He could not love us more. He could not love us more because He has put His whole self into our making.

3. *We are made of God's love.* God is the source of all that is or can be. Nothing can be if God does not sustain it. And where His will is He is. Therefore, it is clear: We are made not just *by* God, but *of* God, out of His love. In creating, God gave of His very being. This was proclaimed when Jesus gave of his very life.

4. *God suffers with us.* Not like human parents who must imagine their child's pain, God knows our pain for all that it is. He feels it with us in the vastness of His compassion, and in order to accompany us in the work of life which He has given us.

The Life of Christ

Since Jesus was sent to teach us the way, the truth, and the life, we should expect his life to provide a model of the life to which we ourselves are called.

Of course, the cross alone is *the* model of Christian life. We too are called to give up our lives, all at once or day by day in countless little sacrifices. And, just as the cross made possible the resurrection, so too our deaths will make possible our own resurrection. In other words, *we give our life back to God and He will give it back to us in a glorified form.*

Nonetheless, though the cross is *the* model of Christian life, all of Jesus' life was crafted to encourage all who follow him.

He was born poor.

His parents were not important people.

He lived far from centers of civilization at the time.

His human father died when he was still young.

Supporting his mother, he was an anonymous laborer almost all his life.

As an itinerant preacher, he got a late start.

He had no patron. He got no "break."

When finally he started preaching, he was misunderstood. (The people thought he was talking about an earthly kingdom — and this was all they wanted.)

When finally he started making disciples, he got opposition (from the religious establishment). He was especially opposed by the Pharisees because they were jealous of their power, envious of his popularity, legalistic, and bound by tradition.

He was betrayed by someone he had trusted (Judas).

He was abandoned by the rest of his friends (the apostles).

He was denied by the person he had appointed to lead his Church (Peter).

He was the subject of lies and condemned unjustly.

He was also the victim of apathy (by Pontius Pilate).

He was rejected and scorned by people he had helped.

He suffered spiritually (in the garden).

Practicing Faith

He suffered physically (on the cross). Crucifixion was the common form of execution. On the cross (on which he was naked), he was also humiliated and ridiculed.

Finally, he died; his movement dead, he appeared utterly defeated. But, as it turned out, he was utterly victorious.

Why was Jesus asked to live such a life? So that if we are betrayed, abandoned, or condemned unjustly, we will not feel that we are worthless. So that we would know that God understands anything we ever suffer. So that we would know that, like Jesus, we can conquer any adversity if only by accepting it.

Comments on the Beatitudes

From the Gospel of Matthew (5:1–12):

How are the poor in spirit — the depressed — blessed? No one will appreciate heaven better.

How are those who mourn blessed? Their pain testifies to the goodness of the person who has died. Surely God would never let this person go.

How are meek blessed? They have nothing to prove.

How are they blessed, those who hunger and thirst for righteousness? In a deliberate and full-time way, they are doing with life what life is for.

How are merciful blessed? Even beyond the fact that they will receive mercy, they have showed a love they did not have to show.

How are the clean of heart blessed? They can always be themselves.

How are peacemakers blessed? They get peace.

How are the persecuted blessed? They get to be like Jesus.

✠

About the "woes" in Luke's version of the beatitudes (6:24–26):

Woe to the rich because they have learned to need too much.

Woe to the full because they no longer appreciate anything.

Woe to those who are always laughing because all too often they are laughing at others.

Woe when all speak well of you. This has become another need. And what do you have to do so that all will continue to speak well of you?

The Our Father

Our Father, who art in heaven — "our" father, and not just our God but our loving provider.

hallowed be thy name — in other words, "holy" be thy name; and I will try not use it in vain.

thy kingdom come — in other words, take us to heaven now.

thy will be done on earth as it is in heaven — in other words, if we are not ready to go to heaven now, let Your plan for us be followed.

Give us this day our daily bread — in other words, give us what we truly need; and I will try not to confuse what I need with what I want.

forgive us our trespasses as we forgive those who trespass against us — in other words, I will try to be as understanding with others as You are with me.

and lead us not into temptation — in other words, knowing my own imperfection, I pray that I will not be too severely tested; and I will try to be compassionate to those who have not been as fortunate so far.

but deliver us from evil — in other words, deliver us from the imperfection of this world; thy kingdom come.

Amen.

✠

For thine is the kingdom, the power, and the glory, now and forever. In other words, heaven is Yours; heaven is You; and this is Your greatness.

Why Do We Hail Mary?

"Let it be done to me as you say" (Luke 1:38).

We honor Mary because of her acceptance of God's will.

Jesus, of course, is *the* model of Christian acceptance; he accepted even death. But Jesus knew why he was asked to accept death. He was doing the Father's will, but he was also doing what he himself believed in.

Mary accepted what she did not understand. She did not know why she had to go through what was happening. She accepted it solely because God sent it. In this, her example is even more applicable to our lives than that of Jesus. After all, the hardest things to accept are the things we do not understand.

The Hail Mary

> Hail Mary, full of grace, the Lord is with you.
> Blessed are you among women
> and blessed is the fruit of your womb, Jesus.
> Holy Mary, Mother of God, pray for us sinners,
> now and at the hour of our death.* Amen.

---

*The last line of the "Hail Mary" was added long after the original taken from the Gospel of Luke (2:28). The phrase "Mother of God" was meant to contradict the thinking of those who held that since Jesus was son of God and son of Mary he was really two persons.

Practicing Faith

In other words: Blessed are you Mary, because you accepted what you did not understand solely because the Father sent it. Blessed am I if I can do the same.

The Seven Sacraments

For all intents and purposes, the word "sacrament" means "sacred sign." It is something we can see, particularly an action, which God through the life of Jesus gave the Church in order to speak to His name.

That God has ordered certain signs to speak for Him is no mystery. We need signs to speak to one another. There are some things you cannot say with words alone. This is also true in church.

Though each of the sacraments is an official act, each has several spiritual meanings. For example:

"Baptism," the act by which people are received into the Church, involves water. It is meant to remind us of the bath that makes us feel like new. Of course, professing faith, or re-professing it, makes us feel the same. The baptism of infants, who are now said to be freed from sin, is a reminder that sin is self-centeredness. They are "freed" in the sense that they have formally embarked upon the road to love.

"Confirmation," where people baptized as infants are now given a chance to speak for themselves, is a reminder of the importance of decision, the one way we *can* gain faith by an act of the will.

Beyond the community's need for structure and official leadership, God gives some "holy orders" because He wants His people to receive His truth from a real voice, His assurance from a real smile, and His love from a real embrace. But all God's people are called to share their faith, and they do this best by living it.

"Confession" helps us to believe that we have gotten a completely new start. After all, if we confess, it is clear that we have learned from whatever happened, turning it from something bad into something good. In confessing, we have dealt with the matter in the way that God has given us to do so. There is nothing else to do or think about. It is in this sense that sins confessed are said to be "erased."

"The anointing of the sick" is done to assure the sick that God will take care of them no matter what. The fact that it often helps people feel better physically is a reminder of the intimate connection between physical and spiritual health.

"Marriage" is a wonderful sacrament. What represents God better than a person? What represents God's love better than the deeply personal and passionate love of a man and a woman, especially when they demonstrate their love in their commitment to one another? After all, you can die for a stranger, but you would willingly share the rest of your life only with someone you love for who this person is. This is the kind of love that God feels for each of us.

The "Eucharist" is the richest sacrament of all. It is the meal we share to remind ourselves that *we were made to be a family.* It is a re-presentation of the moment when Jesus, revealing his decision not to run, accepted the cross to teach and show us love. It blesses the communion where God's love is presented in a way we can see, receive personally in order to remind each of us that God is talking to "me," and even eat whereupon it becomes part of us, reminding us that we can never lose God's love. And much, much more....

Five Meanings of Mass

Though there are more, we can easily distinguish five meanings of Mass:

As a gathering, and therefore a sacrifice, on the part of Christian people, Mass is an act of thanksgiving.

As a gathering of the Christian people for the purpose of thanksgiving, Mass also makes possible "asking"; it is what the Church does to pray in petition.

As a gathering of the Christian people around a table, Mass is the meal which the Church shares to be a family in faith.

As a re-presentation of the last supper, Mass is also a re-presentation of the cross, and the meaning of faith and love, and also of God's love for us.

As a sacrament — an action that God commissioned — Mass is also God's way of giving us something we can see (and receive and even eat) that presents to us His love.

How Mass Re-Presents the Cross

The Mass is God's way to present to us once again the love He first showed to us on the cross. It was well conceived for this great purpose. After all, Jesus may have died on the cross, but he gave up his life the night before, at the last supper, when, in the blessing of the bread and wine, he revealed his decision not to run away knowing that his enemies were coming to arrest and ultimately kill him. This was the moment at which Jesus gave up his life, and Mass presents it as perfectly as it can be. We have all that we could possibly bring together. We have the table, the bread, and the wine. We have a person ordained to represent Jesus every day in every way, who uses the very same words. And the people are real disciples. We have everything that

Practicing Faith

was there at the first last supper. We are going to see that moment when Jesus gave up his life — God's way of showing us that He could not love us more.

Three Liturgical Moments

At Mass there are three liturgical moments.

The first is the consecration of the bread and the wine. We re-present Jesus' decision not to run and thus remember his crucifixion.

The second is the breaking of the bread, when we remember Jesus' death on the cross three hours later.

The liturgical moment of Jesus' resurrection is communion. We say this for four reasons: (1) As something which is given, communion is a reminder that the resurrection experience was sent to the apostles; it was not something they just happened to see. (2) As something that is felt by us interiorly, communion is a reminder that the resurrection was not something that was just "seen"; rather it was something that left no doubt about what God wanted to say. (3) As a reminder of the experience that restored life to the apostles — it certainly restored life to their faith — we are reminded that communion is meant to do the same for us. Finally, (4) as the moment that certain of Jesus' followers were given authority, communion is also the moment that we are recommissioned to be apostles, that is, "witnesses."

Four Reasons to Come to Church

The following are four reasons to come to church:

First of all, we owe God. We owe God everything. And there is nothing we can do to pay Him back. After all, everything we have or ever will have comes from Him. Therefore, there is nothing we can give Him that He didn't give us first. All we can do is to thank Him, and only by our actions can we show that we are really grateful.

Second, He asked us to. But He did not ask us because He needs our thanks. God is God; He needs nothing. God wants us to give Him thanks for our sake — so that we will remember who is God and who are the creatures, and wherein our salvation lies.

Third, *we were made to be a family*. We were made such that our lives are richer in every way when they are shared. Our faith is stronger when we share it. (Mine is stronger because of others, and others' faith is stronger because of mine.)

Finally, we come to church because of what happens in church — the prayers, the readings, the singing, even the preaching. These are meant to inspire and to form, and always to remind.

Thus, to the person who says "I pray on my own" or "I can be a good person without coming to church," the Church responds: Coming to church is not about the idea that we can only pray in church or that to be a good person you have to come to church. Coming to church is about understanding that we were made to be a family and all that this implies.

Besides, people can pray on their own, but they cannot have the Eucharist.

They can think on their own, but they are not being challenged, consoled, or taught.

They may be good people, but they are not doing as well as they could.

Besides, they would not have learned what faith they have were it not for countless people who came to church, and in so doing sustained it.

Five Values of Confession

Confession comes from the fact that a community needs to have rules about those things that are essential to its life. If people break these rules, they put themselves outside the communion of the group. If they are sorry about this and want to return to communion, they need to be reconciled with the community. But since we are talking about only the most serious matters, it is fair to say that we may never face the necessity of confessing, not even once in our lives.

There are, however, occasions when we may profit from going to confession. These involve the "values" of confession. There are five:

First of all, confession gives us something to do to express our sorrow and make up for our sin.

Second, confession makes us examine our lives. After all, in order to speak about our lives, we have to think about how we are living. When we speak about it, we have to confront it. We may be asked a question. Moreover, since confession is about confessing, the confessor is absolutely bound by the "seal,"* and since God already knows the truth, we have no reason to add to our sins by lying.

Third, confession gets a response. Moreover, the person who responds is a student of faith; he hears from the hearts of many people, and he is committed to be objective in his response.

Fourth, at the end of our confession, we hear words of forgiveness. Sacramentally, these are words from God. To confess in prayer is to imagine these words — and to hope they were spoken.

Finally, to confess is to put our sin behind us. After all, if we confess, it is clear that we have learned from whatever happened, turning it from something bad into something good. In confessing, we have dealt with the

---

*The "seal" of confession is the priest's promise of secrecy. There are absolutely no exceptions.

matter in the way that God has given to us. There is nothing else to do or think about. It is in this sense that sins confessed are said to be "erased."

Comments on the Calendar

Faith is best celebrated in sync with the year, the great cycle in which all of us live. The Christian year revolves around two great feasts — Christmas and Easter.

Christmas, or Christ's Mass, always December 25, is the celebration of Jesus' birth. December 25 was chosen as Jesus' birthday because by this date the days are finally getting longer. Light is finally coming (back) into the world. Celebrating Jesus' birthday on this day is thus a wonderful reminder that faith is a light; it is the truth that lets us see differently and live a better life.

Easter, the word derived from Æster, the goddess of Spring, is the celebration of Jesus' resurrection — his appearance to his apostles after his death. The date of Easter changes. It is the first Sunday after the first full moon after the first day of Spring. This dating of Easter is based on information in the New Testament. The continued use of this method of dating Easter is a reminder that we *have* historical information about the death and resurrection of Jesus. The fact that the resurrection happened in the Spring allows us to use this feast as a celebration of the return of life in general.

Of course, as the celebration of the birth of a baby, Christmas is also a celebration of life, while Easter is symbolized by light. As a matter of contrast, Christmas celebrates a birth, while the events surrounding Easter celebrate a death.

Both Christmas and Easter are preceded by seasons of preparation. The preparation for Christmas is called "Advent," from the Latin for "coming," while the season of preparation for Easter is called "Lent," from the German for "lengthening," as in days.

Advent has a twofold character. It begins with our anticipation of the second coming, that is, the transformation of the world, and progresses toward our specific preparations to celebrate the first coming — Christmas.

Lent also has a twofold character. It begins as our yearly churchwide retreat in search of our own rebirth in faith and progresses toward our specific preparations to celebrate Jesus' death and resurrection.

For Christmas, we prepare primarily by waiting and hoping. Meanwhile, we reflect on the meaning of Christmas — not just that Jesus was born but that Jesus was born poor and this was the just the beginning of a life in which he was to suffer anything that we might go through. This way we might know that just as Jesus conquered adversity by accepting it, so can we.

Since the cross stands in the way of our celebration of Easter, Lent is a time of austerity and spiritual work. This helps us to see that, for us too, the cross is the road to glory.

How to Have a Really Happy Advent

Advent is primarily a time of waiting. It is not supposed to be hard. Therefore, to have a happy Advent, all you have to do is check off the following:

1. Use the darkness. Use the long night and, where it happens, the cold to help you be happy to be home. Be quiet, that is, silent. This is what Advent "waiting" is all about. Soon you will experience yourself, your God, His love, and also the truth of all we believe. Let Christmas help you to look forward, and in so doing get a glimpse of heaven. This is what Advent "hoping" is all about.

2. Have a wreath to help stay focused on the season.* See the increasing light of the wreath as a reminder of the reason for the date of Christmas — the

---

*An Advent wreath consists of four candles to be lit one by one on and after the four Sundays of Advent. Three of the candles are usually purple or dark blue, while one is rose or pink. This odd candle is first lit on the third Sunday in Advent because by this day, regardless of the day of the week on which Christmas happens to fall, the season is at least half over. The four candles also symbolize the traditional four thousand years before Christ and are therefore a reminder of how fortunate we are to have lived in this time of light.

fact that by this date increasing light is coming back into the world, that faith is light; it is the truth that lets us see differently and live a better life.

3. Send greetings, being aware that words and symbols communicate the greatest gifts that we can give — love, appreciation, encouragement, reminders of our faith.

4. Remember that Christmas presents are what we do for Jesus on his birthday — we show his love to those we happen to love also.* Keeping this in mind allows us to love twice, and it spares us from needing to be thanked or to get something back that was just as good as what we gave. Remember that the gifts you make and the things you promise are the most beautiful gifts of all.

5. See your Christmas tree as a vote of confidence that the life, not only in nature, but also in you, that is, the joy of your youth, will be more than back the moment you come downstairs on the morning of heaven.

6. Let your little manger help you to reflect on the meaning of Christmas — not that Jesus was born but that Jesus was born poor and this was the just the

---

*This is the reason that Christmas gifts are said to be given by Santa Claus, St. Nicholas, a bishop from the 200s and a famous anonymous giver.

beginning of a life in which he was to suffer anything that we might go through.

How to Make a Really Good Lent

A really good Lent is a really good idea. Not only does a really good Lent lead to an especially joyful Easter, but, even more importantly, it helps us grow spiritually at a time when, in most parts of the world, the oncoming Spring and also the inspirational celebrations of holy week are also working for us.

Inspired by Jesus' forty days in the desert before he assumed his public life, and beginning on Ash Wednesday (see below), a really good Lent consists of doing something in the three traditional areas — prayer, fasting, almsgiving (see Matt. 6:1–18). Of course, counting our time and energy, whatever we do is some form of sacrifice.

In terms of prayer, there are two basic options — public and private.

Public prayer is with others; or it is something to which we go — to church or some other holy place (every day or X times a week). One might make the Stations of the Cross. A person might participate in a Lenten lecture series, or make a pilgrimage.

Private prayer means time — giving God time (at least ten to fifteen minutes every day).

The time can be spent in personal (from the heart) prayer, formal prayer like the Rosary, an examination of conscience, quiet time (to see where it goes), or spiritual reading (such as a chapter a day of one of the gospels).

Fasting means giving up food or something else.

By ancient tradition, Lent also involves periodic abstinence from meat.*

Almsgiving means charity.

Although almsgiving is most obvious when we give money, it also involves the giving of our time and energy, and even of ourselves.

We could take on a special project for the benefit of certain others, a special group, or the entire community. Taking on a clean-up, a fund-raiser, or a letter-writing campaign, for example.

---

*We abstain from meat on Ash Wednesday and Fridays in Lent for five reasons:

1. In most places, meat is a luxury.
2. For most people, to abstain from meat is a sacrifice.
3. Not eating some specific food is a sacrifice we can make together.
4. Not eating some specific food on a particular day helps us to think of that day as special.
5. Not eating meat is a gesture of respect for the flesh of Christ crucified.

We could commit ourselves to use words to build people up. We could commit ourselves to look for opportunities to say something encouraging to someone we would not otherwise notice. This way, by the end of Lent, we have taught ourselves to be more sensitive to those around us.

Beyond all this, since Lent is our preparation to celebrate not just the resurrection but also the cross, it is a great time to reconcile with others, whether that means that we must ask for forgiveness or give it.

Three clarifications:

If we have chosen something especially difficult, and it seems that we could use a weekly day off, this day ought to be Sunday, or Saturday night. (Indeed, Lent is really forty-six, not forty days, for the simple fact that the six Sundays are not counted.) If there are other days we would like to take off — for example, a birthday that falls during the season — we ought to declare this to ourselves before the season starts; otherwise reasons may multiply and soon become excuses.

During Lent, we are not encouraged to give up things that we really need for a healthy, happy rhythm of life. Neither are we encouraged to do something that would in effect penalize others.

Finally, we should never feel good about doing something for Lent that we ought to be doing anyway.

Lent is only forty-six days; Lenten practices are meant to be extraordinary.

Twelve Reasons to Give Things Up

There are twelve good reasons to give things up:

1. To give things up is gratitude, to God, for all that He has given us and all that He has promised. Since God needs nothing from us, all we can do is thank Him. And not just with words because talk is cheap. Tradition suggests sacrifice because in sacrifice, especially when others who themselves might thank us are not being served directly, it is easier to feel that we are doing something for God. Of course, in sacrifice *we* gain. After all, in order to sacrifice out of gratitude, we have to think about the things for which we are grateful.

2. To give things up is to show God — and ourselves — that we do not live for this world only. A person who lives for this world only cannot let anything go. If instead we show ourselves that we believe in heaven, we make our faith grow.

3. To give things up is a means of love. To give up our time, our energy, our money, is now to have more

Practicing Faith

for others. (We have *not* made a sacrifice if we give up one thing we want in order to get another.)

4. To give things up is a motive of love. When we give up things, we understand better the life of those who have less. For example, if we give up food and thus feel hunger, we can better understand the plight of those who are hungry all the time and not by choice.

5. To give things up is to learn not to take them for granted. Those who have experienced hunger never again take their food for granted. They never fail to enjoy it — even if it is not exactly what they wanted. To give up our favorite food is to make sure that it remains our favorite food.

6. To give up food completely for an extended time or on a regular basis, that is, to fast, is to become not only leaner physically but also spiritually; in other words, we think more clearly and feel more alive.

7. To fast is also to experience our dependency. To eat on time all the time is to give oneself the illusion of self-sufficiency, whereas to feel hunger is to realize that we depend on something bigger than we are to keep us alive. In the last analysis, this means God.

8. To fast is also to allow our bodies to begin dying. It is to experience our mortality and to be reminded

of the importance of doing well with life while we still have it.

9. To give up certain things, like cigarettes or some television, is to learn to live without them. This is worthwhile whether or not something is in itself bad for us. After all, the less we need, the freer we are.

10. To give up certain things, like coffee or alcohol, is to find out whether or not we are becoming hooked. (If we find that we cannot give them up easily or happily, then we have another project.)

11. To give up things is to practice willpower. It is to practice keeping our beliefs foremost in our minds. It is to practice saying "no" to our body so that when it really matters we are ready.

12. Finally, to give up things, and then experience the joy of getting them back, reminds us that joy does *not* come because we always have the best of everything. If we always have the best of everything, we get tired of it, no matter what it is. We need to look for more and more. This will lead to self-destruction. Joy comes when things are special — when we do not have them all the time. Anything rare will do. And the more rare, the more joy. This makes clear that joy is available to everyone.

Love the Year

The following is one of the most enriching rules of life you will never forget: Love the year.

Experience the weather. Feel the sun and the cool night air; see the beauty in the sky; experience a storm as a sign of God's power.

Experience the seasons. Better yet, anticipate them; appreciate that we are soon to find ourselves in a new world without having to travel. Experience the diversity in the length of day and the special beauty in each season. Do things that can be done only in season.

Pay attention to the universe. Watch the progress of the moon and the planets. Try to be aware of special spatial events. Look up often so you will better see the hand of God.

Work for a Merry Christmas and a Happy Easter. Have a good Advent; make a good Lent. Keep Christmas and Easter traditions, and do so one by one in order.

Acknowledge the holy and holi-days. Do something different if you are free. Do (or talk about, or sing, or eat) something special even if you are not free.

Have and keep anniversaries. (And you don't need to tell the whole world about all the anniversaries you keep.)

Celebrate your victories big and small, and those of your friends and family.

Have projects; have spiritual projects. Watch what can happen, however slowly, with even a little effort over the course of 365 days.

Recognize a year of living as the accomplishment which it is.

Make plans, and anticipate, a Summer that will separate this from next year.

✠

The following was inspired by Love the year: "Love the day."

See waking up as the gift which it is. Not only has God given you another day, you are bound to take steps toward heaven that could not have taken place on any other day.

Be renewed with every bath or shower. As you experience the symbolism behind baptism, be reminded that you get a new start with God whenever you want one.

Enjoy your daily rituals, or at least their results.

Allow your morning's hot beverage to be a consolation. Let it remind you that even though you soon have to face the world, you will not be facing it alone.

Pay attention to the differences that identify each day of the week.

Practicing Faith

Have a supper that is also a celebration of life and family.

Let nightfall be a promise of peace.

Be in bed as an experience of peace.

Be reflective so that you will be able to say, "I lived today" at the end of every day.

Give some time to God.

A Practical Creed

God made us for life in heaven.

The way to heaven is a life of faith and love.

God guides us according to His plan for everything He sends into our lives.

We are going to share heaven as a family where all of us are going to be richer for the holiness of each of us.

Jesus was sent to teach the truth, to found the Church, and to accept the cross on which he taught and showed us love.

The Eucharist is the meal we share to be God's family, and it is also God's way to show us again and again the love He showed us first on the cross.

The rest of the life of Jesus was planned to show us that faith can conquer any adversity.

A Daily Prayer

Dear God,

Help me to remember that I was made for heaven
so I can live with what I do not have
and dream my dreams in joy.

Help me to remember that the way to heaven
is a life of faith and love
so I will know what I should do and do it.

Help me to remember that You are guiding me
in everything that happens to me
so I can love myself as You love me
and live my life in peace.

Amen.

About the Author

Robert J. Cormier is a preacher, theologian, part-time missionary, and pilot. He lives in Newark, New Jersey, where he is minister to the Spanish-speaking community of St. Rose of Lima, and the Portuguese-speaking community of St. Aloysius. He is the chaplain of several local schools. He is also chaplain at the local state prison, spiritual counselor at the local drug and alcohol rehab, and president of Project Live — a leading institution for the care of the mentally ill. In addition, he serves the English-speaking community of Sacred Heart Chapel in Kearny, New Jersey, and spends his summers ministering to indigenous people in Western Guatemala. A Catholic priest of the Archdiocese of Newark, Father Bob grew up in Cranford, New Jersey, studied theology in Rome, and served as a deacon in Thailand. Besides aviation, his avocations include mountaineering and sailing, and he plays the conga in the St. Rose parish band.

OF RELATED INTEREST

Robert J. Cormier
A FAITH THAT MAKES SENSE
Reflections for Peace, Purpose, and Joy

A whole new concept of faith!

This collection of simple reflections takes the elements common to many faiths and offers them in a way that will indeed make sense to almost everyone.

0-8245-1817-9, $17.95 hardcover
0-8245-1875-6, $10.95 paperback

Richard Rohr
EVERYTHING BELONGS
The Gift of Contemplative Prayer

Revised & Updated!

Richard Rohr has written this book to help us pray better and see life differently. Using parables, koans, and personal experiences, he leads us beyond the techniques of prayer to a place where we can receive the gift of contemplation: the place where (if only for a moment) we see the world in God clearly, and know that everything belongs.

0-8245-1995-7, $16.95 paperback

Ronald Rolheiser
AGAINST AN INFINITE HORIZON
The Finger of God in Our Everyday Lives

In this prequel to *The Holy Longing*, Rolheiser offers further insights into the benefits of community, social justice, sexuality, mortality, and rediscovering the deep beauty and poetry of Christian spirituality.

0-8245-1965-5, $16.95 paperback

Henri Nouwen
LIFE OF THE BELOVED
Spiritual Living in a Secular World

When Nouwen was asked by a secular Jewish friend to explain his faith in simple language, he responded with *Life of the Beloved*, which shows that all people, believers and nonbelievers, are beloved by God unconditionally.

0-8245-1184-0, $15.95 hardcover
0-8245-1986-8, $14.95 paperback

Please support your local bookstore,
or call 1-800-707-0670 for Customer Service.

For a free catalog, write us at

THE CROSSROAD PUBLISHING COMPANY
481 Eighth Avenue, Suite 1550
New York, NY 10001

Visit our website at
www.crossroadpublishing.com
All prices subject to change.